The Italians
and the Holocaust

THE ITALIANS AND THE HOLOCAUST

Persecution, Rescue, and Survival

SUSAN ZUCCOTTI

Basic Books, Inc., Publishers

NEW YORK

Library of Congress Cataloging-in-Publication Data
Zuccotti, Susan, 1940–
  The Italians and the Holocaust.

  Includes bibliographic references and index.
  1. Jews—Italy—Persecutions. 2. Holocaust, Jewish,
(1939–1945)—Italy. 3. World War, 1939–1945—Jews—
Rescue—Italy. 4. Italy—Ethnic relations. I. Title.
DS135.I8Z83 1987   940.53'15'03924045   86–47738
ISBN 0–465–03622–8

To Emilia Levi, three years old,
a "curious, ambitious, cheerful, intelligent child,"
whose parents managed to find water on the deportation train
to bathe her on the eve of her arrival at Auschwitz,

and

to all the other children who shared her fate

CONTENTS

Contents

ACKNOWLEDGMENTS

THIS BOOK could not have been written without the help of two outstanding scholars at the Centro di Documentazione Ebraica Contemporanea (CDEC) in Milan. Liliana Picciotto Fargion, director of research, shared with me the most recent results of her work in Holocaust statistics, much of it still unpublished. She brought documents, books, articles, and photographs to my attention, read my nearly completed manuscript, and offered invaluable suggestions. I have never met as generous a scholar, and I am profoundly grateful.

At an earlier stage in my research, Michele Sarfatti brought me the hundreds of documents of survivor testimony on file at the CDEC, and helped me understand the dimensions of the story. Some of the testimony was written immediately after the war. More was written in 1955, on the occasion of the tenth anniversary of the liberation. Italian Jewish Community leaders at that time wanted to honor Italian non-Jews who had rescued Jews during the German occupation, and they asked survivors to write their stories and nominate potential honorees. Additional testimony was written between 1955 and the present, as more survivors were contacted and encouraged to record their experiences for posterity. Altogether, the documents offer precious insight into patterns of rescue and survival in Italy, and I am grateful to Liliana Picciotto Fargion, Michele

Acknowledgments

Sarfatti, and the entire staff at CDEC for making them available to me.

Historians, archivists, and librarians at many other institutions were also helpful. I would like to thank Professor H. Stuart Hughes at the University of California, San Diego, for his encouragement and attention to my manuscript. Professor Robert O. Paxton at Columbia University I thank for his teaching and support. Raleigh Trevelyan kindly answered my questions, even though I was a total stranger. Archivists and librarians assisted me in a variety of ways. I would like to express my gratitude to the many men and women, most of whose names I never knew, who placed at my disposal the resources of the New York Public Library, Columbia University libraries, the YIVO Institute for Jewish Research, and the Leo Baeck Institute in New York City; the Holocaust Memorial Council and the National Archives in Washington, D.C.; the Wiener Library in London; the Associazione nazionale ex-deportati politici in Milan; and the Associazione nazionale partigiani italiani and the Istituto Luce in Rome.

Many individuals agreed to speak with me, reviving old memories and opening old wounds. Among these, I especially thank Laura Erbsen, formerly of Trieste but now living in New York City; Giorgina Nathan and her husband Winston Burdett in Rome; Massimo Medina in Genoa; and Gastone Orefice, from Livorno but in New York at the time of our interview. Also, many friends thought enough of my work to refer me to these sources. I am grateful to Tobi and Max Frankel for putting me in touch with Laura Erbsen; to Don Hewitt for his trans-Atlantic telephone call to Giorgina and Winston Burdett; to Giovanna and Andreina Zuccotti for the introduction to Massimo Medina. All of these people believe that the story of the Holocaust in Italy must be remembered.

The kindness and consideration of many other friends and family members contributed to this book. Barbara and Donald

Acknowledgments

Zucker made possible my trip to Yad Vashem, and I thank them for their generosity. Israel and Elli Krakowski and Ulo and Ethel Barad shared with me their unbearably painful memories of the Holocaust in Poland and Austria, and focused my attention on similar horrors in Italy. Paul Selver and Lloyd Kaplan carefully read my manuscript, to its great benefit. Lenora Silvers performed numerous technical tasks of manuscript preparation, always cheerfully. Anna DeLaney typed and retyped. I am very grateful to these good friends and special people.

My parents Jane and Ralph Sessions, my mother-in-law Gemma Zuccotti, my aunt Barbara Dill, and my aunt by marriage Rina Mandaro deserve particular thanks, for without their help I could never have completed my research. My children Gianna, Andrew, and Milena have been long-suffering and patient with a mother who was often harassed and preoccupied. Above all, I thank my husband John Zuccotti. He read and studied my manuscript as carefully as any editor and gave me his support and encouragement when I most needed them. He spent days and weeks alone while I was doing research and writing. I know he did it out of love, and I am grateful. But he did it also because he shares my determination that the story of the Holocaust be told and retold, that we who were young then shall not forget, and that new generations of children like our own shall learn, reflect, and try to understand the inconceivable.

PROLOGUE

T HE FAMILY NAME Nathan is familiar to most Italians. Students still read of Sara Levi Nathan, devoted admirer, friend, and correspondent of Giuseppe Mazzini, the leader, with Cavour and Garibaldi, of Italian unification. Students still learn of Sara's even more famous son, Ernesto Nathan, the first Jewish mayor of Rome, elected in 1907.[1] But Italians know little about Giuseppe Nathan, Ernesto's son and Sara's grandson. His is a story they may prefer to forget.[2]

During the 1920s and most of the 1930s—the era of triumphant fascism in Italy—Giuseppe Nathan was a prosperous and respected Roman banker. He lived in London for many years, representing the Bank of Italy, marrying an Australian woman, and raising his children to be bilingual. But his heart belonged to Italy. It was an allegiance that nearly cost him his life.

Unlike his father, Giuseppe Nathan had no interest or time for politics. He was neither favorable nor opposed to fascism. He was too busy with his young family, his travels, and his career. The career flourished until 1938. In that fateful year, Mussolini's racial laws suddenly decreed that Giuseppe Nathan could no longer work for the Bank of Italy. His children could not attend public schools. He could not have a Catholic maid in his house. He could not even list his name in the telephone directory. The illustrious name of Nathan now scarcely existed, because it was a Jewish name.

In desperation, Giuseppe Nathan moved his young family to Australia late in 1938. Restless and nostalgic for both work and Italy, he set out alone for Europe, via the United States. In San Francisco, his reputation and experience as a banker held him in good stead, and he received excellent career offers. He had arrived at the turning point of his life. Yet late in 1939, as war was breaking out in Europe, he decided to refuse all offers, return to Italy, and send for his family. He missed the land of his forefathers. He did not want to make his way outside it.

The Nathans lived in wartime Italy for several years, under constant police surveillance. Their passports were confiscated. Giuseppe's career was finished and his income vastly reduced. Sorrow and anxiety turned to terror on September 8, 1943, however, when the Germans occupied the country of their former ally. Immediately aware of the danger of arrest and deportation, Giuseppe fled with his family to a village in the Abruzzi.

After the Allied landings at Anzio in January 1944, the Nathans returned to Rome, believing that the city would soon be liberated. They even managed to hitch a ride home on a German truck. The Nazis and their Italian Fascist cronies were arresting all Jews, but despite their fanatic racism, they could not recognize their victims by sight.

The Nathans naturally could not live at home in Rome. Giuseppe hid his wife, an enemy national, and his children in private homes or convents. He himself found refuge in a monastery. In the spring of 1944, an Italian spy informed the Nazis that fugitives were hiding in the monastery. During the raid that followed, Giuseppe hid behind heavy draperies. His shoes protruded, and he was caught. He spent four days under relentless interrogation at Gestapo headquarters in the Via Tasso. He was then transferred to the infamous Roman prison of Regina

Coeli. He was fortunate to have arrived there after the Ardea-
tine Caves massacre on March 24, 1944. Regina Coeli had
been emptied of its male Jewish prisoners at that time, to help
fill the SS order for victims to be shot in reprisal for the killing
of 33 German SS police during a partisan attack in Rome's Via
Rasella. The Nazis demanded a ratio of 10 Italians to be killed
for every German. They executed 335 men and boys—5 more
than ordered. Of the 335, 77 were Jewish.[3]

Giuseppe Nathan remained at Regina Coeli, awaiting transport to Auschwitz. Again he was fortunate. The Allies arrived
in June, before enough Jewish prisoners could be assembled to
make a new transport worth the effort. Liberated, shaken, and
in need of care, he checked into the Grand Hotel. On the
registration form, he wrote his previous address: Regina Coeli.

The Nathan family survived the war and eventually resumed
a semblance of normal life. Giuseppe Nathan was reemployed
at the Bank of Italy. He died in 1952, at the age of sixty-five.

The adventures of Giuseppe Nathan typify, in almost every
respect, the experiences of Jews in Italy during World War II.
Italian Jews were rarely as famous as Giuseppe's father, but
most were assimilated middle-class professionals. Most had
lived in Italy for generations and were profoundly patriotic. All
were devastated by the racial laws in 1938, and many emigrated
or converted. All were forced into hiding during the German
occupation, although the majority did not recognize the danger
as quickly as the Nathans. Most, like Giuseppe, survived with
the help of Italian rescuers, often men and women of the
Church. But more than 6,800 did not survive.[4] Like Giuseppe,
they were betrayed by informers. Unlike him, they were forced
into cattle cars and shipped to the gas chambers and ovens of
Auschwitz.

About 85 percent of the 45,200 Jews in Italy during the
German occupation lived to see liberation.[5] This book exam-

ines the nature of the Holocaust in Italy, where the survival rate was among the highest in occupied Europe. The statistic cannot be taken for granted. After all, as late as the second half of the nineteenth century, Italy hosted some of the most oppressive Jewish ghettos in the world. After a few decades of unification, emancipation, and democratic government, the country fell under authoritarian Fascist rule in 1922. Then in 1938, Italy became officially anti-Semitic, and non-Jewish Italians were informed that Jews were their enemies and the cause of all evil. Furthermore, Italy became Hitler's willing ally in war in June 1940, and a full partner in a crusade that included, among other objectives, the goal of making Europe *Judenrein* —free of Jews.

After the German occupation of Italy, Benito Mussolini's puppet regime continued to cooperate fully with the Nazis. The political manifesto of the new regime declared in November 1943, that Italian Jews were enemy aliens. A police order in December 1943, called for the internment of all Jews. Adolf Eichmann sent highly experienced teams of Jew hunters to Italy, as he did to all occupied nations. Thousands of Italian Fascists, from conviction, careerism, or sheer greed, were eager to help them. The Holocaust in Italy was executed with ferocious determination. How did so many manage to survive it?

Yet, strangely enough, quite the opposite question might be asked. About 15 percent of the Jews in Italy during the German occupation did not survive the Holocaust. This book asks how more than 6,800 people could have been rounded up and deported to be gassed from a country that, despite its nineteenth-century ghettos and the promptings of its Fascist rulers, had no significant anti-Semitic tradition. Jews had lived in Italy since before the Christian Era. In 1943, they were proportionately few, thoroughly assimilated, and physically indistinguishable from their Christian countrymen. It should not have been difficult for them to hide. They lived in the shadow of the

Vatican, in close proximity to the moral and spiritual leader of the Catholic world and the supreme teacher of Christian precepts of brotherly love and the sanctity of human life. And the Holocaust began much later in Italy than in most other European countries, so that Jews should have been aware of the danger and quick to flee. In Rome, the danger period from September 1943 to June 1944 lasted only nine months; in most of central Italy, it continued three or four months longer; in northern Italy, it existed until April 1945. A maximum of twenty months, yet 15 percent of Italy's Jews were destroyed. How could it have happened?

The answers to both questions lie with the people involved. The majority of Jewish Italians were brave, resourceful, individualistic, nonsubmissive, and determined to survive. A tiny minority were terrified, unimaginative, passive, and unable to act to save their own lives. Many non-Jewish Italians were anti-German, anti-Fascist, and prepared to help all fugitives who came their way. Italian men and women of the Church stood in the forefront of the rescue effort, even while the man in the Vatican resolved not to be involved. Sympathetic priests and nuns were joined by doctors, lawyers, government officials, peasants, and housewives. Meanwhile, a small minority of non-Jewish Italians served the Nazi occupiers of their country, hunted fugitives at the side of the Gestapo, and betrayed their Jewish neighbors.

This book examines the behavior of men, women, and children, Jewish and Christian alike, living in the shadow of death. Jews who survived owed their lives to their own personal initiative, Christian help, and large doses of good luck. The tragedies of those who died can be traced occasionally to lack of initiative, but more often to betrayal by Christian neighbors. In occupied countries where the Nazi goal was total Jewish extermination, survival rates were determined by the personal decisions of Jews, the responses of Christian countrymen in both their public and private capacities, and luck. In Italy, those factors determined that 38,400 Jews would survive while more than 6,800 would die.

The sad but ultimately favorable balance suggests that, for the most part, the decisions of Jews in Italy were wise and correct. The responses of many Italian non-Jews, in the absence of support from their government, were decent and courageous. We cannot explain why individuals are good or bad, wise or foolish, courageous or cowardly. We can, however, try to understand the context in which decisions are made. We can also ask ourselves whether we, in our country essentially free from anti-Semitism, might, under similar pressures, make decisions as wise and courageous as many Italians did.

The Italians
and the Holocaust

1

The Holocaust
Comes to Italy

EVEN before the Italian declaration of war against the Allies on June 10, 1940, sixty-eight-year-old Marshal Pietro Badoglio, chief of the General Staff, had warned that the army was not prepared. Events confirmed his judgment. Only a few days after the Italian attack on Greece on October 28, 1940, the army was in retreat. In January 1941, the British defeated Marshal Rodolfo Graziani in North Africa, advancing three hundred miles into Libya and taking more than 100,000 prisoners. Italy lost Eritrea, Somalia, and Ethiopia by April, along with another 250,000 prisoners. Prime Minister Benito Mussolini, the individual most responsible for reckless military decisions and poor planning, unceremoniously retired both Badoglio and Graziani.

In March 1941, the Germans bailed out the Italians in North Africa. In April, they conquered Greece, where Italians had been bogged down for five months. Mussolini in turn sent 200,000 men to fight beside the Germans in Russia in June. A euphoric year and a half of Axis victories followed. Defeats at El Alamein and Stalingrad at the end of 1942, however, abruptly ended illusions of victory, and Italians began to perceive the truth. Anglo-American troops landed in Morocco and Algeria in November 1942, and the pincers closed tightly around Axis forces in Tunisia. Meanwhile, 115,000 Italians died and 60,000 were captured on the frozen Russian steppes. Those who straggled home again spread demoralizing tales of defeat and German abandonment of their Fascist ally on the battlefield.

Conditions deteriorated rapidly in Italy. Food shortages and rationing made the war highly unpopular. Allied bombing took an increasingly devastating toll. Thousands of urban refugees sought safety in the countryside, disrupting production and straining resources. Disgruntled workers staged frequent work stoppages. Finally, in March 1943, a strike of Fiat workers in Turin spread across northern Italy despite vicious police efforts to stop it. It ultimately affected more than 100,000 workers. The strike convinced industrialists and businessmen that Mussolini was no longer in control. Allied landings in Sicily in July brought military leaders to the same conclusion. Mussolini's fate was sealed.

On July 25, 1943, the diminutive and indecisive King Victor Emmanuel III finally heeded the advice of businessmen, military officers, and Fascist moderates. All hoped to disassociate themselves from Mussolini and salvage their lives, property, and a shred of honor from the wreckage of dictatorship. Emboldened by a Fascist Grand Council vote of no confidence in Mussolini the previous day, the king summoned the prime minister to his villa, stripped him of authority, and arrested him. In a broadcast to the people that evening, the king announced that Badoglio was returning from retirement and would head the new government. He added that the war would continue.

The news stunned the Italian people. Benito Mussolini had, after all, ruled Italy since October 1922, when thousands of Fascist thugs had threatened to tear Rome apart unless the young Victor Emmanuel III appointed their leader prime minister. Twenty-one years later, many Italians could remember no other government. Yet, after three years of an unpopular war, most greeted Mussolini's fall with jubilation. Huge crowds cheered in the streets. Eager young men destroyed Fascist symbols and monuments and searched out petty Fascist tyrants for beatings, imprisonment, or worse.

But not everyone rejoiced during that confused July. Many Fascist sympathizers remained lurking in the shadows. They knew that a permanent transition from dictatorship to democracy would not be easy. They consoled themselves with schemes for a future reckoning of accounts. Meanwhile, the war continued.

Among those who greeted the fall of fascism with jubilation and immense relief was a community of about 37,100 Italian and 7,000 foreign Jews. [1] Their number had been considerably larger—the census of 1938 recorded more than 47,000 Italian Jews, or slightly more than one-tenth of 1 percent of a population of forty-five million. It also listed more than 10,000 Jews of foreign nationality. [2] But the fascism that in 1922 seemed remarkably free of anti-Semitism had not, in the end, done well by its Jews. The racial laws introduced in 1938 required, among other things, the expulsion of all foreign Jews. While this objective was never achieved, the outbreak of war in 1940 resulted in the arrest and detention of thousands. Foreign Jews in miserable internment camps were "permitted" to build their own huts and dig their own wells, if they could secure tools and materials.

The Italians and The Holocaust

For Italian Jews, the racial laws decreed that they could no longer practice their professions, own property over a certain value, send their children to public schools, or marry or employ non-Jews. Throughout the country, thousands of doctors, lawyers, teachers, and civil servants were suspended. Military officers with a lifetime of service were suddenly retired. Children were withdrawn from school. With the outbreak of war, many Italian Jews were also subjected to forced labor.[3] Under the pressures of the racial laws, at least six thousand Italian Jews had emigrated and about the same number had converted by July 1943.[4] Those remaining hoped for better days.

Their optimism was not unjustified. Badoglio was expected to restore the full rights of all Italian citizens and release foreign Jews from internment camps. He would end harassment, anti-Semitic posters, graffiti, and the sacking of synagogues. But Badoglio was still at war. His dangerous and suspicious ally needed to be reassured, or deceived, about Italy's intentions. While he did release most political prisoners, excepting Communists but including Italian Jews, he did little to mitigate the racial laws. The Jews—and the nation—waited. Through the hot summer of 1943, as the Allies raced across Sicily and approached the Italian mainland, the Germans waited as well, and prepared for the day they knew was not far off.

Badoglio, in fact, would have only forty-five days. The real turning point in the lives of all Italians was not July 25 but September 8. At 6:30 that evening, Allied Commander in Chief General Dwight D. Eisenhower announced Italy's unconditional surrender. At 7:45, Badoglio confirmed the armistice and instructed the Italian army to lay down its arms before the Allies but to "react" to attack "from any other quarter." Because the U.S. Fifth Army was not scheduled to land at Salerno until the next day, Allied forces on the Italian mainland on September 8 were limited to General Bernard Montgomery's British Eighth Army disembarking at the

Straits of Messina, at the southernmost tip of the peninsula. There were virtually no Allies available before whom the Italian army could lay down its arms. There were, however, at least eighteen German army divisions throughout Italy, with more poised on the frontier awaiting the Italian surrender.[5] The entire Italian army found itself abandoned without realistic instructions on how to deal with its former ally. Because the Germans were naturally determined that no Italian territory, manpower, or weaponry should fall to the enemy, armed confrontations occurred throughout the country.

Some heroic Italian officers after the September 8 armistice resisted German capture. On the island of Cephalonia, thousands of officers and men followed Badoglio's instructions and "reacted" to attack. When they finally surrendered to the Germans, they were all summarily executed. In Corfu, after an equally heroic three-day resistance, seven thousand surrendering Italian soldiers were killed. Nor was resistance limited to distant fronts. General Don Ferrante Gonzaga, commanding Italian forces at Salerno, refused to surrender his weapon to the Germans and was immediately shot down.[6] And there were others.

In the absence of instructions and a declaration of war against the Germans who surrounded them, however, most Italian officers and men decided that their best option was to disappear. Throughout Italy, hundreds of thousands of young soldiers abandoned uniforms and weapons, put on civilian clothes, and went home. Many ultimately joined the partisans, particularly after it became clear that the Germans and their Fascist sympathizers would hunt them down and treat them as deserters. Many others were captured immediately. About 640,000 Italian officers and men spent the remainder of the war in German prison camps, where 30,000 died.[7]

* * *

The Italians and The Holocaust

Italian civilians greeted the events of September 8 with mixed emotions. Official hostilities, at least, were over, but Italy was an occupied country. Germans were much more formidable as conquerors than as allies, particularly for the Jews. For despite the hardships and degradations of the racial laws, it must be remembered that until September 8, 1943, the Jews in Fascist Italy had fared better than Jews in almost any other country in Nazi Europe. Even in unoccupied France, laws in 1940 and 1941 similar to the Italian racial laws of 1938 had limited or banned Jews from most professions and expropriated their property. Foreign Jews in unoccupied France were systematically thrown into wretched internment camps. Then in July 1942, fully four months before the Germans entered the unoccupied French zone, Vichy agreed to release foreign Jews to the Nazis for deportation. At least seven thousand were delivered by August.[8] Such a thing never happened in Fascist Italy before the German occupation. On the contrary, Jewish refugees continued to seek and obtain sanctuary in Mussolini's Italy until the very day of the armistice. In addition, Italian army officers and diplomats occupying Croatia, Greece, and parts of southern France protected Jews from German demands for deportation.

In German-occupied countries, the nightmare of the Holocaust was in full swing. Deportations began in Belgium, the Netherlands, and occupied France in 1942. In a single action in Paris, on July 16 and 17, 1942, French police rounded up 12,800 foreign Jewish men, women, and children. Deported to Auschwitz, about 30 returned after the war.[9] By the end of 1942, about 42,500 Jews had been deported from France to Auschwitz, including 6,000 children.[10]

Even during the Badoglio interlude, Italian Jews dependent on censored news services knew little of these horrors, or regarded radio reports from the BBC and neutral countries as Allied propaganda. At the very worst, they thought, deporta-

8

tion to the East meant work camps and hard labor. Such a fate was certainly undesirable, but it could never happen in Italy. Italy had been Germany's ally. Indeed, after the Germans rescued Mussolini on September 12 and set him up at Salò on Lake Garda as the titular head of the new Italian Social Republic, Italy became Germany's ally again. Italian Jews were enlightened, educated, and assimilated. They were good and patriotic citizens. Why would anyone bother them?

Within a few days, the Jews had their answer. On September 16 in Merano, a beautiful mountain resort town near Bolzano, twenty-five Jews, including a child of six and a woman of seventy-four torn from her sick bed, were arrested by Nazis, interrogated, beaten, and deported. Only one of the twenty-five survived the war.[11] On September 18 in small northern Italian villages near the French border, about 349 Jewish refugees from France were also caught by the SS. These men, women, and children, originally from countries throughout occupied Europe, had fled to France before 1940, then to Vichy France, then to the Italian-occupied French zone, and finally, after the Italian armistice, to Italy itself. About 330 of the prisoners were deported back to France and ultimately to Auschwitz. Nine survived the war.[12]

Elsewhere that tragic September, SS troops invaded the tranquil shores of beautiful Lago Maggiore, on the Swiss frontier. In idyllic villages like Stresa, Arona, Baveno, and Meina, they hunted Jews as one might track wild game. They murdered forty-nine victims on the spot, throwing their bodies into shallow graves or into the lake. They raped one young girl in front of her mother, before shooting both.[13]

The worst atrocities occurred in Meina, a village on the lake between the more famous tourist towns of Arona and Stresa. The train between Milan and the Simplon Pass leading to Switzerland stops there today, and the traveler can see quiet streets and vine-covered hills dropping to the water's edge. But in 1943 Meina's tourists were refugees, Jews and non-Jews, Italians and foreigners, fleeing the bombed-out cities of northern Italy. The tiny village, beautiful, full of vacant hotel rooms off-season, and conveniently near the Swiss border, was a perfect haven. Sixteen Jews, many from war-torn Greece, took lodgings in the Hotel Meina. They sought safety in the very nation that, with significant German help, had defeated their own. Someone informed the Nazis.

On September 16, one week after the German occupation, the SS stormed the hotel. They seized a family of six from Salonika, including the mother and father, the seventy-six-year-old grandfather, and the children aged fifteen, twelve, and eight. They kept this family and ten other victims under guard for a week, debating, apparently, what to do with them. Finally, on the night of September 22, they marched out three separate groups of four people each. They shot each victim in the back of the neck and tossed the bodies into the lake.

At dawn, only the elderly grandfather and his three grandchildren remained under SS guard at the hotel. The parents had already been taken away. The four terrified victims waited that entire day. During the afternoon, one of the children found the courage to go onto a balcony and call to a woman below, "Where are Mommy and Daddy?" The woman replied gently that she thought they had been taken away for an interrogation. Finally, at nightfall, the SS came for the remaining prisoners. A witness at the hotel later reported hearing the grandfather scream and beg for the lives of the children. The children died as brutally as their elders. The SS auctioned the belongings of the victims on Meina's public square. Lago Maggiore gave up only one of the sixteen corpses. [14]

And so the Holocaust came to Italy. The war that began in June 1940 had caused young men to be drafted and sent to die in Russia or Africa or the Balkans. With that war had come air raids, and civilians killed in their beds. But three years later, the war acquired a new dimension. After the German occupation of Italy, children and grandparents could be shot in the back of the neck merely because of their religion.

A non-Jewish Italian maid seeking information about the fate of her Jewish employer, just murdered by the SS near Meina, was told she would never see them again. She objected timidly that they were good people. An SS man replied, "Not good people. Jews, who are the ruin of Europe." [15] This was the war that came to Italy on September 8.

2

Italy's Jews

THE JEWS of Italy trace their roots back hundreds of
years before the barbarian invasions that contributed so much
to the "mixed blood" of their persecutors. In fact, if one wishes
to speak of "pure blood" in Italy at all, one thinks first of the
Jews. Long before the destruction of the Temple in Jerusalem
by Titus in A.D. 70—indeed, long before the heirs of Saint
Peter proclaimed Rome the holy city of Christendom—a Jewish colony had settled along the banks of the Tiber. The histo-
rian Josephus records at least eight thousand Jews living there
in the year 4 B.C. The synagogue well preceded the Vatican.
Many more Jews arrived during the imperial period, when the
community peaked at about fifty thousand.[1] This population
exceeded the entire Italian Jewish community in 1943.

During the Christian Era and the Middle Ages, Jews in Italy
experienced a grim succession of restrictions and persecutions,
relieved by brief interludes of calm. The Italian Renaissance,
from roughly the early fifteenth to the mid-sixteenth century,
offered some respite. Jewish scholars worked with Christian

humanists in an atmosphere of mutual tolerance and respect. Jews exiled from Spain and Spanish-controlled territories settled in Italy at this time, bringing rich variations of liturgy, language, and customs which they carefully preserved apart from their Italian coreligionists.

The Counter-Reformation shattered tolerance and introduced the phenomenon of the ghetto. The word "ghetto" is said to derive from the Italian word "getto," meaning metal casting and referring to the iron foundries in the part of Venice where Jews were first confined in the sixteenth century. From there, ghettos quickly developed in most major Italian cities and throughout Europe. Jews were confined to these ghettos, with few exceptions, for over two hundred years.

Ghetto life was difficult and degrading. [2] In many cities, Jews could work only as street peddlers, hawkers, ragpickers, dealers in second-hand merchandise, and pawnbrokers. Women, not allowed to make and sell new clothes, mended old clothes for their men to sell. Poverty was endemic. The housing was wretched, and the stench appalling. Scarcely able to contain an ever-growing population, the walled enclaves became festering labyrinths of dark and narrow streets lined with tall, rickety structures. Buildings soaring upward to meet the pressure for shelter sometimes collapsed altogether.

Ghetto Jews faced the problems of poverty, malnutrition, and disease by organizing self-help associations for every category of daily life. There were societies to help the poor, provide dowries, aid in childbirth, tend the sick, finance funerals, and provide for orphans. Jews dealt with problems of isolation and despair by educating themselves. Illiteracy was unusual in the ghetto at a time when it was the general rule outside. But ghetto residents could not so easily resist the threat from beyond their walls.

Jews in Italy paid crushing taxes and tributes, with no hope of appeal. Police could enter their homes and confiscate household goods at will. Incited by perpetual charges of ritual murder, police could search the ghettos for missing children. On Saturdays, they could look for and punish friendly Christians lighting the Sabbath fires and thus illegally "working" for Jews. In the Papal States, where the ghetto system was most repressive, police also sought out Jews evading their obligation to attend lengthy conversionist sermons, where earnest priests, sometimes themselves converted Jews, lectured for hours. Christian churchmen regularly examined their captive audiences to determine that no one had stopped his ears or fallen asleep.

If a Jew of any age expressed, or even seemed to evidence, an interest in conversion, the outside threat magnified itself a hundredfold. The "convert" could be held indefinitely in a special house of catechumens, regardless of his age or the wishes of his family. On the contrary, if the "convert" was head of a household, his whole family could be held as well, or children could be taken from their mother. Such stories may help explain why Italian Holocaust survivors, when writing of priests who helped them, invariably add, "and they made no attempt to convert me." The current reader would take that for granted, but not so in 1943.

Involuntary baptism was another terror for ghetto Jews until well into the nineteenth century. Any Catholic layman or laywoman was qualified to perform a valid baptism. If he or she baptized a Jew, regardless of age or ability to consent, that person was a Christian and could not live in a non-Christian community. As recently as 1858 in Bologna in the Papal States, a seven-year-old boy baptized at age one by a servant girl was seized from his family, paraded through the ghetto, baptized again, and not returned, despite appeals from his desperate parents and protests from around the world.[3]

The Enlightenment sounded the death knell of the ghetto, but in some parts of Italy the ancient institution took nearly a century to pass away. In Hapsburg-controlled Lombardy and Trieste, the Grand Duchy of Tuscany, and the Duchy of Parma, reforms began well before the French Revolution. In nearly all Italian cities, Jews were temporarily emancipated during the Revolutionary and Napoleonic Eras, only to be sent back to the ghettos during the Restoration. Full permanent emancipation did not come until the unification of Italy: in 1848 in Piedmont, in 1859 or 1860 in the states that joined Piedmont to form Italy, and in 1870 in Rome. Jews correctly attributed their new-found freedom and equality to the House of Savoy, secular nineteenth-century Liberalism, and their new nation. In gratitude, they firmly endorsed all three institutions.

Many Jews contributed to the struggle for Italian unification. In Venice, the famous patriot Daniele Manin, elected president of the new republic when it tried to rid itself of Hapsburg rule in 1848, was half Jewish. Many Venetian Jews eagerly supported him. In Rome, the city with the most repressive ghetto in Italy, three Jews were elected to the National Assembly of the new republic proclaimed after Pope Pius IX fled in 1849. Three others sat on the City Council, and two served on the Committee for Defense. [4] Jews fought and died in the unsuccessful defense of Rome against French and papal troops in 1849, in battles against the Hapsburgs in Lombardy in 1848, 1849, and 1859, and with Garibaldi's gallant Thousand against the Bourbons in Sicily in 1860. They served with the Italian troops who breeched the walls of Rome at the Porta Pia Gate and seized the city from its papal defenders in 1870. In the process, they helped unify the peninsula and opened the last ghetto remaining in Western Europe.

After emancipation, Italian Jews immediately began to appear in positions of prominence and distinction. Isacco Artom, for example, served as private secretary to Prime Minister Camillo di Cavour in Piedmont in the 1850s. He later became the first Jew in Europe to fill a high diplomatic post outside his own country. Giacomo Dina directed Cavour's official publication, *Opinione*. Two Jews became city councilors in Rome in 1870, as soon as the ghetto was dissolved. Three Jews were elected to the first parliament of a nearly united Italy in 1861. Nine sat in 1870, after Venice and Rome were included. Eleven sat in 1874.[5]

The prompt appearance of Jews in prominent positions after emancipation suggests that a large segment of the Italian population had not shared the prejudices of its Old Regime rulers. Discrimination in the nineteenth century had indeed been an artificial imposition, intimately tied to broader attempts to restore pre-French Revolutionary regimes. Many Italians, and particularly those anticlerical Liberals who became the governing elite in the newly united nation, had disapproved. Each time revolutionary crowds assaulted ghetto walls and opened gates between 1820 and 1848, witnesses described mass jubilation by Jews and non-Jews alike. But the rapid integration after emancipation also testifies to the character of the Italian Jewish community itself. Italian Jews were not foreigners. They looked, dressed, and spoke like everyone else. And above all, they were educated. In 1861, only 5.8 percent of all Italian Jews over the age of ten were illiterate; the figure for the Catholic community was 54.5 percent.[6] Italian Jews were well prepared for the opportunities that emancipation offered.

Complete integration was nevertheless not without its difficulties. In 1873, for example, the possibility of the appointment of a Jew as minister of finance aroused so much fear of a revival of Catholic anti-Semitism that the candidate quietly withdrew.[7] By 1891, however, Luigi Luzzatti, a member of a prominent and highly patriotic Venetian Jewish family, was appointed to the same position without protests. He served until 1892, and then from 1896 to 1898 and again from 1903 to 1906. In 1910, he was appointed prime minister. This, it might be noted, occurred twenty-six years before the first Jewish prime minister served in France.

Luzzatti was not the only Jew to reach a pinnacle of power. Salvatore Barzilai, a fiery Irredentist orator and journalist from Trieste, was elected to the Chamber of Deputies in 1890, remained for eight terms, served in the cabinet before and during World War I, and was a member of the Italian delegation to the peace conference at Versailles after that war. Claudio Treves and Giuseppe Emanuele Modigliani, elder brother of the painter Amedeo Modigliani, served as Socialist deputies for many years before, during, and after World War I. Ernesto Nathan, a Freemason, became mayor of Rome in 1907, only thirty-seven years after the ghetto had been opened. Leopoldo Franchetti, sociologist and author of numerous foreign colonization schemes, served as a conservative senator for many years before committing suicide in despair after the Italian debacle at Caporetto. And Baron Sidney Sonnino, the converted (Protestant) son of a Tuscan Jewish landowner, served as finance minister and foreign minister, and finally in 1906 (and again from 1908 to 1910) as prime minister. These are only the best-known Jewish politicians; there were many others. By 1902, the Italian Senate of about 350 notables appointed by the king included six Jews. By 1920, there were nineteen. [8]

The Jewish contribution to the military during the late nineteenth and early twentieth centuries was also outstanding, particularly in contrast to other European nations. One might compare the fate of Captain Dreyfus to the glittering career of Giuseppe Ottolenghi, Italy's first Jewish general appointed in 1888. Ottolenghi served as an instructor to the future Victor Emmanuel III. In 1902, at a time when in Germany no professing Jew could even hold a commission, he became a senator and the minister of war.

A few years later, fifty Jewish generals served in World War I. Among them, General Emanuele Pugliese became the most highly decorated general in the Italian army. General Roberto Segre, an artillery commander, designed the artillery defenses on the Piave that checked the Austrian offensive there in June 1918 and decisively shattered enemy morale. General Guido Liuzzi was commander of the War School. General Angelo Modena distinguished himself in the Libyan War and in World War I, concluding his career with an appointment in the late 1920s as president of the Supreme Army and Navy Tribunal. These generals were joined by thousands of other Jewish officers and enlisted men. More than a thousand won medals for valor. [9] The nation's youngest gold-medal winner, Roberto Sarfatti, killed in combat at the age of seventeen, was Jewish, as was the oldest, volunteer Giulio Blum.

Italian Jews also made significant contributions in business, banking, and insurance, in the professions, and in education and the arts. Lodovico Mortara, for example, was president of Italy's highest court in the 1920s. Vittorio Polacco was a highly respected professor of law at the Universities of Padua, Modena, and Rome from 1885 until the 1920s. In 1930, 8 percent of all university professors were Jewish. [10] And in literature, two of Italy's finest novelists before World War II, Italo Svevo, born Ettore Schmitz, and Alberto Moravia, born Alberto Pincherle, were Jewish and half Jewish respectively.

Not only had many Italian Jews reached positions of prominence by the early years of the twentieth century, but most others had assimilated and were leading full and varied lives. In his perceptive memoirs, a prosperous Modenese lawyer named Enzo Levi follows the transition from isolation to integration through several generations of his own family, from 1858 until World War II. [11] In the process, Levi reveals changes in the society as well.

In 1858, Enzo Levi's great-grandfather was forced to flee the Duchy of Modena with all his worldly goods in the back of a wagon. He had refused the duke's demands to change his name and convert to Catholicism. Enzo's own father, then a one-year-old child, rode in the wagon. The Levis returned a year later, when the duke was in turn expelled and the duchy was united to Italy.

In keeping with the new age of opportunity, Enzo's father became a successful lawyer and a fervent patriot and monarchist. "In my family," the son remembers, "as in many bourgeois families, especially Jewish ones, there really existed a blind veneration for the House of Savoy." During the Dreyfus Affair, Levi's parents assured him that such a thing could never happen in Italy, where Jews were protected by the king and the constitution. After the assassination of King Umberto by an anarchist in 1900, the Levi family grieved as if the loss were personal. They seemed much like any other middle-class Italian family, with slight differences.

Enzo Levi's parents were religious, and they observed the Sabbath, the holidays, and the dietary laws. Their friends were mostly Jewish. Their son recalls how difficult it was immediately after the abolition of the Modena ghetto for Catholics and Jews to get to know each other. They did not share the same holidays, and they could not even eat together easily. Of about fifteen marriages in Enzo's family in the 1880s, only one was mixed. That one was much criticized even though it was a civil marriage requiring no conversion.

Enzo Levi was born in 1889. Like most middle-class children, whether Jewish or Catholic, he attended public elementary and high schools. Unlike the Catholic students, however, Levi has vivid memories of being tormented by a group of boys, always the same ones, because he was Jewish. He reluctantly learned to fight, but he could not understand either how they knew he was Jewish or why they disliked Jews. He adds that the boys were "from a bad element," and that he had many Catholic friends.

By the time Levi was approaching adulthood around 1910,

The Italians and The Holocaust

Jews and Catholics began mixing much more easily. The appointments of Luzzatti as prime minister and Ottolenghi as minister of war were taken by Jews as signs of the end of anti-Semitism. Levi's own children suffered virtually none of the anti-Semitism that he himself had known. At the same time, however, Italian Jews began to abandon their heritage. Mixed marriages in Levi's generation were more common than Jewish ones. The children of mixed marriages generally became Catholics. Levi himself married a Jewish girl, but they had a civil ceremony and did not circumcise their son. Levi became an atheist. He did not go to the synagogue or believe in the religious institution, but he retained, like so many, a profound belief in the relevance of the ethical concepts of Judaism to modern life.

Levi's account of his drift away from Judaism is echoed in the writings of many middle-class Jews who were young in the 1920s and 1930s. Emanuele Artom, for example, the twenty-nine-year-old Jewish partisan captured by the Germans and tortured horribly until he died in 1944, recorded in his famous diary that he had little interest in Judaism until he was about eighteen.[12] Sion Segre Amar, a young Jewish anti-Fascist arrested and tried before the Fascist Special Tribunal in a much-publicized case in 1934, remembers that Yom Kippur was the only holiday he respected and observed.[13] Carlo Modigliani, an industrial engineer, mathematics professor, talented amateur pianist and composer, and air force pilot in World War I, records that until the racial laws he "had forgotten completely about being Jewish."[14] His father, a successful musician, was an atheist; his mother was religious. Carlo went to the synagogue irregularly in Ferrara, learning to read Hebrew and say the prayers as a child, but he ceased all participation when he moved to Milan at the age of eighteen.

In an amusing reminiscence in 1962, Salvatore Jona summed up what it meant to many to be Jewish in the 1920s:

"For the young it was a matter of going to the temple a couple of times a year, of not eating pork *at home,* and of not telling one's good mother that one would willingly marry a nice Catholic girl." [15] And what did one do to avoid displeasing one's mother with the prospect of a mixed marriage? "As long as mamma lived, a Christian girl remained only the beloved. After mamma died, sometimes, a decent period of mourning having passed, the beloved became a spouse." Under such circumstances, Italian Jewry seemed destined to decline and disappear within a few generations.

The high degree of assimilation and the decline of religious observance by the mid-1930s should not be misconstrued as an abandonment of Jewish values. Italian Jews were Italians through and through, but many remained aware and proud of their Jewishness. Enzo Levi, even as an atheist, retained a deep respect for Jewish ethical concepts. Emanuele Artom, in some of the most moving entries of his diary, expressed the same respect, even reverence, for his cultural and ethical heritage. Ora Kohn from Turin, whose parents did not work on Saturday but allowed their children to ride the streetcar and attend school that day, nevertheless remembers that her family "had this sense of values, a sense of tradition." She adds, "Our sense of Jewish identity came from the family. It was not from observing holidays, because we weren't holiday-observing people." [16] Gastone Orefice, the only Jew in his class at the public school in Livorno, says the same. "My grandfather didn't care very much [about religion] and my father didn't care and my mother as well. But we were Jews. This was important to us. Our culture, our talking at home was Jewish." [17]

The most impressive proof of Italian Jews' ties to their heritage came after the racial laws, when conversion became a tempting method of avoiding discrimination. The racial measures of 1938 did not apply to offspring of mixed marriages

The Italians and The Holocaust

baptized before the promulgation of the laws (or if born after the laws, within ten days of birth). Individuals with two Jewish parents but baptized before October 1938 were not automatically exempt from persecution, but they could hope for preferential treatment, Vatican protection, and a change in the law. Compounding the temptation, the Church was very cooperative in back-dating baptismal certificates. Under these circumstances, roughly six thousand Italian Jews, particularly those in mixed marriages, converted. [18] Most Jewish families had some relatives who were baptized. But tens of thousands did not yield, although doing so would have allowed them to continue their careers or educations and retain their businesses or lands. They were not observant, but they would not deny their heritage.

If Levi's memoirs err in any way, it is in the portrayal of Italian society as entirely free of anti-Semitism by the 1920s. Levi is not alone in this respect; most Jewish writers confirm his description almost too readily, as if they wanted to convince themselves. Upon reflection, however, and perhaps with the benefit of hindsight, the situation seems more complex. Could a society that had tolerated ghettos as late as 1870 have changed so totally in half a century—in less than a single lifetime? Could Catholics, whose holy mass contained a reference to Jews as the killers of Christ until the reforms of Pope John XXIII, remain entirely immune to such rhetoric? Did the virulent anti-Jewish press campaign and the violent cruelty of Fascist fanatics during the German occupation of Italy come from nowhere, from a society previously free of anti-Semitism? A closer look seems necessary.

Indications of anti-Semitism are rare, but they exist. Ora Kohn, born in Turin in 1921, says, "Most of my friends were not Jewish. . . . Religion had nothing to do with making friends. Occasionally you might find someone who was anti-Semitic, who would be cold when he found out you were Jewish, but it was a big world. There were lots of other people." [19]

Renata Lombroso from Milan, born in 1903, has more unpleasant memories. "My parents had taught me not to say that I was Jewish," she remembers, "but I . . . said it in a loud voice, provoking anti-Semitism. In elementary school, having refused to participate in the Christian religious lessons [refusal was her legal right], I had my first fights with my schoolmates, who waited for me by the exit. . . . Even the teachers showed anti-Semitism, although I was one of the best pupils." One publicly called her "the rotten pear among the good pears," a phrase that she says stayed with her all her life. [20]

If Renata Lombroso's experiences were unusual, other Jewish writers mention being taunted occasionally, especially on Good Friday. Augusto Segre, the son of a rabbi from Casale Monferrato in Piedmont, sums up the situation:

> If, even in my times, when I was a boy [he was born in 1918], sporadic unpleasant episodes occurred involving us, and some religious or laic anti-Semite stumbled upon us . . . many of us were always ready to pass over these little incidents, to minimize them, maintaining that it was not wise . . . to argue with Christians and that it was instead much more important and useful, for the good of all, to keep quiet, pretend nothing had happened, avoid responses that were useless and stupid because they were always damaging to us. In short, we were taught it was necessary to do everything possible not only to avoid being noticed, but to demonstrate always more, through work, through charity, through participation in the political life of the country if possible, that the liberty conceded us was simply justified by so much fervor of Italian patriotism. [21]

The years of Jewish assimilation in Italy extend well into the years of fascism. Mussolini's rise to power in 1922 brought not the slightest change in the process. Indeed, many Jews were loyal Fascists from the start. At least five Jews were included among the 119 Italians who met in a small hall on the Piazza San Sepolcro in Milan on March 23, 1919, to found the *Fasci Italiani di Combattimento*, Mussolini's first national organization and the precursor of the Fascist party. Cesare Goldman, one of these *sansepolcristi*, as they were called, had helped secure the hall. Among the Fascist "martyrs" who died in violent conflicts with Socialists between 1919 and 1922, there were three Jews—Diulio Sinigaglia, Gino Bolaffi, and Bruno Mondolfo. By the time of the Fascist march on Rome in October 1922 and Mussolini's ascent to the office of prime minister, 746 Jews belonged to either the Fascist or the Nationalist party (the two merged in March 1923). Over two hundred Jews claimed to have participated in the march, and officially received special honorary status to prove it. [22] And in addition to the activists, many Jewish businessmen, like their non-Jewish counterparts, helped finance the fledgling Fascist movement.

Jewish involvement with Italian fascism is not surprising. With the exception of many in Rome, most Italian Jews were solidly middle-class, and by late 1921, fascism had become a basically middle-class, antiworker movement. Early revolutionary aspects had declined, leaving as primary goals anti-socialism, union busting, strike breaking, and the restoration of law and order at workers' expense. These objectives pleased both the Jewish and non-Jewish middle classes—conservative men and women who had loyally supported the war and suffered from war-induced inflation, and who now felt threatened by industrial and agricultural workers with their powerful trade unions, their inflation-adjusted wages, and their antipatriotic revolutionary rhetoric. In addition, many middle-class Jews felt more comfortable with fascism's anticlerical strain, a remnant of its radical origins, than with Catholic conservative factions.

Obviously not all, or even most, middle-class Jews were Fascists, any more than most non-Jews. A majority of all thought-

ful, educated adults understood the danger of an authoritarian
regime that employed violence to convince doubters and intim-
idate opponents. A majority of Jewish adults understood the
particular danger of such a regime to themselves, agreeing
quietly with Augusto Segre's father, the local rabbi of Casale
Monferrato, who told his son in the 1920s that "whoever
considers himself truly Jewish will not mix with those people
who are against justice and liberty."[23]

Most doubters and opponents kept their opinions to themselves, but some courageously spoke out. Eucardio Momigliani,
for example, one of the original Jewish *sansepolcristi*, abandoned fascism almost immediately, proclaimed his opposition,
and founded the anti-Fascist Unione Democratica. Pio
Donati, an anti-Fascist Jewish deputy, was twice beaten and
finally driven into exile, where he died alone in 1926. Other
anti-Fascist Jews in exile in the 1920s and early 1930s included
Claudio Treves, Giuseppe Emanuele Modigliani, and Carlo
Rosselli. There were many anti-Fascist non-Jews in exile as
well.

If the presence of Jews among the Fascists indicates again the
thorough integration of Jews into Italian society, it also suggests that Mussolini's movement was as free from anti-Semitism as any other political party in Italy. There were, it will be
noted, no full Jews who remained in the Nazi party after Hitler
came to power. In this respect, fascism was a reflection of the
society at large. Prejudiced individuals existed, but they remained a vocal few. Fascism did not become officially anti-
Semitic until Mussolini chose to make it so, with the racial laws
in 1938.

During the 1920s and 1930s, a number of Jews held important positions in the Fascist government. Aldo Finzi, a pilot
with Gabriele D'Annunzio in Fiume and the only Fascist
among the nine Jews elected to the Chamber of Deputies in

The Italians and The Holocaust

May 1921, became an undersecretary at the Ministry of the Interior and a member of the first Fascist Grand Council. Dante Almansi, a prefect before the march on Rome, served as a vice-chief of police under Emilio De Bono until his forced retirement after the racial laws. Guido Jung served as minister of finance from 1932 to 1935.

These three were only the most important. There were many others. Maurizio Rava was a vice-governor of Libya, governor of Somalia, and a general in the Fascist militia. Renzo Ravenna, a lawyer, friend of Italo Balbo, and former *squadrista* (the name given to fanatical Fascist thugs who in 1920 and 1921 roamed the countryside in armed groups beating up Socialist workers and peasants) was the *podestà*, or appointed mayor, of Ferrara for fifteen years. Ugo Foà, captain in World War I, winner of a silver medal for military valor, lawyer, and Fascist party member after 1932, served as magistrate from 1939 until, like Almansi, he was forced into retirement. And Giorgio Del Vecchio, an eminent professor of international jurisprudence and philosophy, became the first Fascist rector of the University of Rome in 1925.

On a less elevated plane but nonetheless indicative of the Duce's attitudes, Margherita Sarfatti, Mussolini's mistress and influential associate for many years, was also Jewish. Margherita was the editor of the art and literature page of Mussolini's *Popolo d'Italia* and a coeditor of *Gerarchia*, the Fascist party's monthly ideological review. She presided over a fashionable salon of Fascist *prominenti* in Milan for many years, and she liked to think that she had made Mussolini fit for polite society. She was ousted by Clara Petacci, quite another type, about 1936.

The prominent Jewish Fascists were joined by thousands of their more humble coreligionists. Gastone Orefice recalls his grandfather, a successful pharmacist in Livorno, as "a very nice honest person, a very old-style person, and until 1938 he was sure that fascism and Italy were one. When the Fascists told him he wasn't a good Italian anymore and that he couldn't be a Jew and an Italian at the same time, he had problems with himself." [24] There were many honest, nonpolitical Italian Jews who felt the same. Between October 1928 and October 1933, 4,920 of them joined the Fascist party. [25] They represented slightly more than 10 percent of the Italian Jewish population as a whole. The membership percentage of the non-Jewish population was roughly the same.

3

The Racial Laws

ON MARCH 11, 1934, Sion Segre Amar, a young man from Turin, was caught at the frontier town of Ponte Tresa smuggling anti-Fascist literature into Italy from Switzerland. His friend Mario Levi escaped by swimming back across an icy river to safety. According to the hostile press, the dripping wet Levi shouted anti-Fascist and, the newspapers added significantly, anti-Italian insults from across the frontier.[1]

Segre Amar and Levi were Jewish. They were also members of the well-known Giustizia e Libertà (Justice and Liberty), the largest non-Marxist anti-Fascist organization of the period. Giustizia e Libertà had a large proportion of well-educated and high-minded Jewish members—so many, in fact, that Segre Amar later recalled that when he informed Carlo Levi, subsequently famous as the author of *Christ Stopped at Eboli*, of his interest in the group, Levi's comment was, "Alas, another Jew."[2]

Segre Amar's arrest was followed by a roundup of thirty-nine suspects, including Mario Levi's brother Gino, an engineer at the Olivetti Typewriter Company in Ivrea, and his elderly father Giuseppe, a biology professor at the University of Turin. Most detainees were soon released, but of the seventeen held at length, eleven were Jewish. Carlo Levi, then a doctor, painter, and writer in Turin, was held, as was Leone Ginzburg, a future Resistance hero who died in prison during the German occupation. The newspapers covered the Ponte Teresa "conspiracy" with gusto, emphasizing Mario Levi's alleged anti-Italian insult. Also, for the first time in their coverage of anti-Fascist activities, the press stressed the fact that many of the conspirators were Jewish. [3]

None of those arrested were Zionists. Giustizia e Libertà, in fact, had no active Zionist members. [4] The press was not concerned with facts, however, and the Ponte Tresa affair became the focus of a vicious anti-Zionist campaign. The equation anti-Fascist = anti-patriot = Zionist = Jew was repeated over and over again. "Next Year in Jerusalem; This Year at the Special Tribunal" was a headline in Telesio Interlandi's newspaper *Il Tevere* on March 31. "It is necessary to decide," said Roberto Farinacci in his newspaper *Il Regime fascista.* "Whoever calls himself a Zionist has no right to try to retain obligations, honors, benefices, etc., in our country." [5]

The Ponte Tresa affair could hardly have come at a worse moment. Adolf Hitler had become chancellor of Germany a year earlier, on January 30, 1933. Mussolini was proud of his protégé, whose success was another demonstration of the decadence of Liberal democracy. He was disturbed, however, by Hitler's undisguised ambitions in Austria and among German minorities in Italy's own Trent and Trieste. In 1934, Mussolini still regarded Austria as within his own sphere of influence, and he had every intention of resisting German expansion there. He was nevertheless reluctant to alienate Hitler.

One obvious method of mollifying Hitler while yet resisting him was to instigate an anti-Semitic campaign in Italy. Thus

The Italians and The Holocaust

in January 1934, Mussolini unleashed his anti-Semitic journalist friends, led by Telesio Interlandi. A series of anti-Zionist articles appeared. Into that maelstrom came the Ponte Tresa affair. Mussolini must have been rather pleased.

And yet, as quickly as it began, it was over. Austrian chancellor Engelbert Dollfuss was assassinated by Nazis on July 25, 1934, and Mussolini mobilized troops at the Brenner Pass to defend Austria from German attack. Better relations with Britain and France now seemed desirable, and an anti-Semitic campaign was no longer expedient. In September, Mussolini made his wonderful comment, "Thirty centuries of history permit us to regard with supreme pity certain doctrines supported beyond the Alps by the descendents of people who did not know how to write, and could not hand down documents recording their own lives, at a time when Rome had Caesar, Virgil, and Augustus."[6] Anti-Zionist articles ceased. By the time the Ponte Tresa conspirators appeared for trial in November, they were virtually forgotten. Only three—Sion Segre Amar, Leone Ginzburg, and Mario Levi (in absentia)—were actually tried and convicted. They received light sentences and little publicity.

While the reaction to the Ponte Tresa affair revealed the intimate connection between Mussolini's Jewish and German policies, it also unmasked an unexpectedly vocal and vicious anti-Semitic presence in Italian society. Italians who took pride in the religious and racial tolerance of the regime were surprised, but others recalled warning signs that had existed even in the good years. Some remembered, for example, a brief incident in 1928 when an article entitled "Religione o nazione?" in the November 29–30 issue of *Popolo di Roma* criticized a recent Italian Zionist congress and questioned the patriotism of its participants. While the article was unsigned, its author was generally recognized as Mussolini himself. The article prompted a flood of letters from Jews protesting their loyalty to the Duce and the nation. It was a sad harbinger of things to come.[7]

By the early 1930s, skeptics of Mussolini's benevolence toward Jews began to point out that despite the high number of accomplished Jewish scholars and scientists in the country, none had been appointed to the Italian Academy. Mussolini made light of the criticism, assuring an interviewer in 1932 that he was at that very moment considering a Jewish appointment. None occurred.[8]

More alarming was the shadowy existence of obscure anti-Semitic fanatics hovering in the wings awaiting their cue. Chief among these was Giovanni Preziosi, renegade priest, nationalist, and Fascist since 1920. Preziosi published his anti-Semitic newspaper *La Vita Italiana* throughout the 1920s. In 1921, he translated and circulated throughout Italy the infamous "Protocols of the Elders of Zion," a forged document proporting to prove a Jewish conspiracy to dominate the world. Mussolini seems to have detested Preziosi, but Roberto Farinacci was his protector. He also cultivated German Nazi friends who later became useful. As most Fascists considered him a crank throughout the 1920s and early 1930s, however, his role remained minimal until the war.[9]

Among the Fascist rank and file too, there were anti-Semitic elements even in the 1920s. In his memoirs, Augusto Segre remembers several early incidents in his town of Casale Monferrato, east of Turin. In one case, someone put two old rusty gates against a wall facing a café frequented by Fascists, with a sign "Put the Jews back in the ghetto." In another incident, one of the best-known Fascists in town approached Segre's twenty-year-old brother in a café, grabbed his jacket, and called him and all Jews "subversives and Freemasons." Segre himself was also harassed on occasion by Fascist thugs.[10]

On another level, Mussolini's persistent suspicion of Zionism also disturbed many perceptive observers. He regarded

The Italians and The Holocaust

Zionists as "internationalists" or as people with "dual loyalties" —both unacceptable in his increasingly monolithic state. With more justification, perhaps, he also saw them as tinted with Liberal democracy, socialism, and, consequently, anti-fascism. As a result, he was always more sympathetic to Vladimir Zwed Jabotinsky's brand of authoritarian Zionist revisionism than to the official democratic Zionist mainstream. Mussolini also viewed Zionists as instruments of British imperial policy who would facilitate the division and rule of the Palestinian mandate. Only sporadically did he consider that support of Zionism might help extend Italian influence in the Mediterranean. Finally, he feared that support of Zionists would alienate the Arabs, whose good will he hoped to cultivate as part of his anti-British policy in the Middle East.

Throughout the good years, Mussolini's anti-Zionist suspicions remained dormant. Between July 1934 and the middle of 1936, while he cultivated the Stresa front, hoped for a British and French blessing upon his Ethiopian endeavor, and remained wary of Nazi Germany, Mussolini actually made pro-Zionist statements and held several friendly meetings with Zionist leaders. In December 1934, with the temporary idea that support for Zionism might increase his international influence, he even permitted young Jews from Jabotinsky's revisionist Zionist organization (but not those from official Zionist circles) to study at the Italian Maritime School in Civitavecchia. Jewish students from all over Europe and from Palestine formed a special section at the school, pursuing Hebrew, Palestinian geography, and other related subjects in addition to their maritime courses. Years later, Jewish graduates of the Maritime School became the basic cadres of the fledgling Israeli navy. [11]

In mid-1936, after the Ethiopian sanctions and Italian intervention in the Spanish Civil War, Mussolini decided to burn all his bridges. Soon after the appointment of his pro-German son-in-law Galeazzo Ciano as foreign minister, Mussolini allied Italy unequivocably with Hitler. Anti-Zionism was immediately rekindled with a vengeance. This time, the flames grew into an intense, undisguised anti-Semitism. One of Italy's first profoundly anti-Semitic pamphlets, Alfredo Romanini's *Ebrei-Cristianesimo-Fascismo*, appeared in 1936. Later that year, Farinacci's newspaper *Il Regime fascista* began to attack not only Zionists but all Jews, claiming that they had not done enough for their country and must put fascism before Judaism. Anti-Semitic graffiti appeared for the first time on the walls of Jewish homes in Ferrara in the summer of 1936. [12] And in April 1937, Paolo Orano's famous book *Gli ebrei in Italia* appeared. The transition from anti-Zionism to anti-Semitism seemed complete as Orano called upon Jews to reject, not just "foreign loyalties," but their entire cultural heritage. They should withdraw from all local Jewish social, educational, cultural, or athletic associations and blend entirely into the anonymous Fascist masses.

While a chronological connection between Mussolini's Jewish and German policies is undeniable, the causal connection is subtle. Mussolini was isolated and anxious for a German alliance after the Ethiopian War and the Italian intervention in Spain, but there is no evidence that Hitler or his top aides ever demanded an anti-Semitic program as the price of German friendship. [13] Mussolini alone bears responsibility for the racial laws. On the other hand, he did not have to be told that an Italian racial policy would please the Führer by demonstrating that the Fascists had cut all ties with Britain and France. Mussolini introduced the racial laws, in part, as a token of the sincerity of his bid for an alliance.

By 1936, an increasingly racist political and intellectual climate at home also influenced the formation of Fascist Jewish policy. To some extent, Mussolini controlled that climate by unleashing his anti-Semitic cronies at appropriate times. But other factors remained beyond his control, and here again German influence appears. Nazi agents operating in Italy in the early 1930s frequently stirred up local anti-Semites and encouraged young pro-Nazi government officials. Bureaucrats who hoped to build their careers on a German alliance were quick to understand the value of an anti-Semitic policy, and tried to push the prime minister in that direction.

Apart from the German influence, many right-wing associations as well as elements within the Church became increasingly anti-Bolshevik during the Spanish Civil War. These forces tended to equate Bolsheviks with Jews. Publications like the Jesuit newspaper *La Civiltà cattolica* and the Catholic University of Milan's journal *Vita e pensiero* began to warn the public of the Jewish danger. [14] At the same time, government officials, ever more conscious of racial issues after the Ethiopian War, began to penalize Italians for sexual contact with blacks. [15] Racism was clearly growing in Italy, independently of the Nazis. Mussolini's decision to adopt a racial policy was consistent with the times.

Once decided, Mussolini mobilized a vast press campaign to marshal public support for the racial laws. Early in 1938, the standard anti-Semitic press became increasingly shrill. Small local newspapers and youth organization publications, especially those most in need of funds and subject to government influence, promptly followed the new line. In August 1938, Telesio Interlandi began his particularly vicious newspaper *La Difesa della razza*, which appeared throughout the country every two weeks until July 1943. Eventually, almost every national newspaper picked up the anti-Jewish theme. [16] Fascist spokesmen, bureaucrats, and rival journalists made life difficult for publications that seemed reluctant to toe the line. Very few resisted for long.

Many press attacks focused on foreign Jews, cited as the cause of housing shortages, high rents, high prices, food scarcities, unemployment, low wages, crowded schools, crime, and every other conceivable social and economic ill. Articles emphasized the pro-British aspects of Zionism, anti-Semitic measures in other countries, and Jewish support for the Loyalists in the Spanish Civil War. The press denigrated all Jewish contributions to cultural and intellectual life, past and present, in Italy and beyond. Indeed, considering the extent of the attacks and the complete absence of published dissent, it is remarkable that Italians remained as skeptical and disapproving of the racial laws as they did.

Radio programs also reflected the anti-Semitic theme throughout 1938. Associations ranging from the Italian Academy and the National Institute of Fascist Culture to university student clubs and local party groups held conferences, seminars, and study sessions. Finally, on July 14, 1938, the infamous *Manifesto degli scienziati razzisti* (Manifesto of the Racial Scientists) was published. The scientists claimed that "the population and civilization of Italy today is of Aryan origin. . . . [and] there exists a pure Italian race. . . . [but] Jews do not belong to the Italian race." The manifesto attempted to provide a scientific justification for the coming racial laws. [17]

The manifesto was a fraud in every respect. Even Mussolini, who understood all too well the German definition of the term Aryan, did not believe its content. Furthermore, the manner of its proclamation was farcical. It was signed by ten "experts," of whom at least four were young university assistants just beginning their careers and vulnerable to political pressure. Only one of the ten had national stature. [18] Worst of all, the original Manifesto of the Racial Scientists appeared with no signatures at all. The list of ten followed several days later!

As a final step in the preparation for the racial laws, the Ministry of the Interior announced in July that the Central Demography Office would become the far more sinister Office of Demography and Race. The new agency was immediately ordered to conduct a census of all Jews in Italy—a task it performed in August.

After Mussolini's softening-up campaign, the actual anti-Semitic measures surprised no one. The first restrictions involved education. Just before the autumn term, the government announced that no Jews could study or teach in public schools during the coming academic year. Elementary schools with more than ten Jewish students were required to establish separate sections and facilities for them. Secondary schooling was not provided, but individual Jewish communities were empowered to organize their own schools if they wished. Jewish students, both Italian and foreign, already enrolled in universities could complete their program, but no new students would be admitted.

Other early restrictions concerned the more than ten thousand foreign Jews recorded by the August census. On September 2 and 3, the government announced that foreign Jews could no longer establish residence in Italy, Libya, or the Dodecanese Islands. Those already in residence were to leave within six months. Worst of all, Jews who had been nationalized after January 1, 1919, lost their citizenship and were regarded as foreigners.

The bulk of the racial laws became official on November 17, 1938.[19] Marriage between Jews and non-Jews was prohibited. Jews were not permitted to own or manage companies involved in military production, or factories that employed over one hundred people or exceeded a certain value. They could not own land over a certain value, serve in the armed forces, employ non-Jewish Italian domestics, or belong to the Fascist party. Their employment in banks, insurance companies, and national and municipal administration was forbidden.

The original November laws also wrestled with the elusive problem of exactly who was Jewish. In a country where intermarriage and religious conversion were common, the inevitable result was confusion. First, in ostensibly the easiest cases, the law decreed that children of two Jewish parents were themselves Jewish, even if they belonged to another religion. That provision, denying as it did the possibility of conversion, antagonized the Church. Next, those with one Jewish and one foreign parent were also declared Jewish, as were the offspring of a Jewish mother and an unknown father. In cases of obvious mixed marriages between Jewish and non-Jewish Italian citizens, children were Jewish if they practiced Judaism or were inscribed in the community. They were not Jewish only if, in addition to having one non-Jewish Italian parent, they had been baptized before October 1, 1938. Furthermore, that non-Jewish parent had to be "pure Aryan," for according to the law, children of a mixed marriage were Jewish if they had "more than fifty percent Jewish blood."[20]

The law ultimately provided for other cases. Children of mixed marriages born between October 1, 1938 and October 1, 1939 were given time for baptism; those born after October 1, 1939 had to be baptized within ten days. Those baptized before October 1938 but subsequently compromised through marriage to Jews were subject to various intricate provisions.[21]

In the attempt to appease opponents of the racial laws, the original November regulations also defined a policy of exemptions for certain categories. The immediate families of Jews killed, wounded, or decorated while fighting in Libya, World War I, Ethiopia, and Spain, along with the families of men who volunteered for service in those wars, might secure exemptions. Individuals and their families who had participated in Gabriele D'Annunzio's occupation of Fiume in 1919, had joined the Fascist party between 1919 and 1922 or during the second half of 1924 (after the murder of Socialist deputy Giacomo Matteotti by Fascist thugs), or had been wounded in the Fascist cause, were also included as eligible exemptees. Finally, individuals with exceptional merit of a "civic nature" (a quality left undefined in the statutes) might secure exemptions for themselves and their families.

All exemptions, however, were subject to limitations. First, they were not awarded automatically, but on a case-by-case basis determined by a special commission of the Ministry of the Interior. Decisions were capricious, to say the least. The family of Memo Bemporad, for example, was denied an exemption despite the fact that his grandfather had supported Garibaldi, his mother's brother had died in combat in World War I, his mother had directed a hospital during the same war and received a silver medal, and his father-in-law had been decorated for service as an officer in two wars. Denial was based on the grounds—accurate, Bemporad hastens to add—that the family had shown no enthusiasm for fascism. [22]

Decisions were usually determined, not on the merits, but by the greed, envy, fanaticism, and, occasionally, good will of those in power. It was not unusual to wait for hours, be forced to return several times, have to pay bribes, and have announcements of decisions delayed for months while the bribes continued. [23] After all that, a favorable decision might be granted to one individual but not extended to the family. Exemptions could also be revoked at any time, without reason or explanation. [24]

Even when secured, exemptions did not cover all the restrictions defined in the racial laws. Exemptees still could not hold a job in a bank or in public administration. They could not teach, and their children could not study in the public schools. They could, according to the November laws, still serve in the armed forces, but on December 22, 1938, military authorities themselves decided to retire all Jewish officers in permanent active service, regardless of their exemption status. [25] Exemptees could, however, hold property without limitation and continue in most professions. By January 15, 1943, the Office of Demography and Race at the Ministry of the Interior had examined 5,870 applications. Of these, they had granted 2,486 and refused 3,384. [26]

The exemption policy may be seen as a reasonable, if badly executed, attempt to recognize Jews who had rendered some special services to their country or to the Fascist cause. Indeed, Italo Balbo, Emilio De Bono, and some other Fascist Grand Council members who disliked the racial laws had argued that exemptions should be granted to the families of all who had served in Italy's wars, and not merely to those who had been killed, wounded, or decorated. A subsequent exemption program, however, had no justification of any kind, and was starkly symptomatic of overall Fascist cynicism and corruption.

On July 13, 1939, the government introduced an Aryanization program, by which a special commission could simply declare arbitrarily that a Jew was not a Jew. Because applicants for Aryanization did not have to prove any personal service record, bribery became the primary determinant of decisions. [27] Even worse, Aryanized individuals received privileges that far exceeded those awarded exemptees under the earlier program. Because Aryanized Jews were no longer Jews, they suffered no disabilities at all. The Aryanization program promptly fulfilled the purpose for which it had been designed, honoring the most corrupt and penalizing by default the most worthy.

In addition to the Aryanization law, scores of other laws, regulations, and decrees appeared in 1939 to supplement the original November program. On June 29, for example, all Jews were prohibited from working as notaries, and only exemptees were allowed to work as journalists, doctors, pharmacists, veterinarians, lawyers, accountants, engineers, architects, chemists, agronomists, and mathematicians. The vast majority without exemptions could practice their professions only among other Jews. Another law prohibited all personal service by Aryans for Jews. Many other 1939 decrees constituted pure and simple harassment. For example, Jews could not own radios, place advertisements or death notices in the newspapers, publish books, hold public conferences, list their names and numbers in telephone directories (operators could give the information orally), or frequent popular vacation spots. The last measure appeared in the summer, when many were already away. They had to come home.

In many cases, local anti-Semitic initiatives exceeded even the national program. Local ordinances frequently denied licenses to small Jewish businesses, shops, restaurants, and cafés. A local decree in Rome revoked the licenses of rag pickers and second-hand clothes dealers. Supplies could be withheld even from legitimate shops. Jewish employees not officially affected by the racial laws could nevertheless be fired on unofficial orders from above. The zeal with which these measures were executed varied from place to place, but the suffering was widespread and acute.[28]

Advocates of the Italian racial laws liked to claim that their brand of anti-Semitism differed from the Nazi variety in two respects. First, they maintained, it was based on spiritual and cultural, rather than biological, concepts. As such, it was consistent with Italian traditions and the teachings of the Church. The truth was rather different. Provisions that refused to recognize conversions, either because both parents were Jewish or because baptism had not occurred before a certain date, clearly treated Jews as a race.[29] On the other hand, provisions that treated the children of mixed marriages differently depending only upon their religion ignored the concept of race. So, too, did provisions granting exemptions on the basis of service or even bribes. In fact, Italian anti-Semitism had no ideological base, but was the product of mindless and cynical opportunism.

Second, advocates of the laws liked to claim that their goal, unlike that of Nazi anti-Semites, was to discriminate, not persecute. The government did not interfere with freedom of worship, Fascists pointed out, and education in principle was not prohibited—the state simply ceased to provide it. Jews retained their right to protection under the law, and they could practice their professions among themselves. The state merely demanded their separation from the rest of society. In fact, however, this was a specious distinction. Inability to practice a trade or profession freely, or even to operate a shop, constituted economic persecution for thousands of unfortunates. It could have been worse, but it was severe enough.

The racial laws immediately affected thousands of people. The more than ten thousand foreign Jews were the hardest hit, for they had been required in September 1938 to leave the country altogether. A mitigating clause in the November laws stipulated that those aged sixty-five and over by October 1, 1938, and those married to Italian citizens by the same date could remain, but all others had to leave by March 1939. By then, 933 had won the right to stay and 3,720 had left—a number that increased, often through threats of expulsion, to 6,480 by September. [30]

Emigrants were simply replaced, however, by thousands of Jewish refugees entering from even less hospitable countries. Italy closed her frontier to German, Polish, Hungarian, and Rumanian Jews in August 1939, but sympathetic Italian border guards often looked the other way. By October 1941, there were 7,000 foreign Jews in Italy, of whom more than 3,000 were fairly recent arrivals. [31] They had no official status, no means of sustenance, no right to remain in the country, and no place to go. Many were placed in internment camps or enforced residence after Italy entered the war.

Among Italian Jews, the racial laws caused, first of all, the abrupt end of jobs and educations. Within a few weeks, about 200 teachers at all levels, 400 public employees, 500 private employees, 150 military personnel, and 2,500 in the professions lost their positions. At the same time, 200 students in universities, 1,000 in secondary schools, and 4,400 in elementary schools were affected. [32]

To ease the economic impact of the racial laws, special clauses provided that pensions, and in cases of brief employment, partial pensions, be paid to those who would have received them upon normal retirement. Also, confiscated property was partially compensated. Professional people could continue to practice within the small and now impoverished Jewish community. Teachers could teach in Jewish schools. These provisions helped many in middle-income groups but were no consolation to small shopkeepers, artisans, and workers —the less affluent lower classes, particularly numerous in Rome. Without economic resources or the means to emigrate, many existed almost entirely on charity from the Jewish communities. Clustered in old ghetto neighborhoods and lacking the money and contacts to secure hiding places, they were the first to fall into the clutches of the SS in 1943.

Many non-Jews benefited financially from the elimination of professional competition and sales of Jewish property and shops. More than 2,500 non-Jews suffered, however, when they lost the personal service jobs they had held with Jewish families. Their complaints went unheeded. Again fascism succeeded in serving the strong and harming the weak.

If the economic impact was harshest among the lower classes, however, the emotional shock was probably greater among the more affluent and assimilated—among those who thought they belonged to Italian society. Nearly 6,000 Italian Jews had emigrated by October 1941—a particularly poignant statistic in light of their veneration for country and king before 1938—and another 6,000 had converted. [33] There were also several suicides among the middle classes. The most dramatic case was that of Angelo Fortunato Formiggini, a highly respected author, journalist, publisher, and early critic of fascism. On November 29, 1938, Formiggini threw himself from the

Ghirlandina Tower in his native Modena, in the expressed hope of demonstrating to all his countrymen the horror of racial laws that persecuted a few. [34] Fabio Della Seta, a young high school student in Rome, also recalled the suicide of a distant relative who had served in World War I and had been unable to bear the racial laws. His regimental band had played a beautiful funeral march, which the Jewish community thought to be a good sign. [35]

The vast majority of assimilated and nonpolitical Italian Jews reacted to the racial laws with shock and disbelief. Particularly poignant is the story of General Ugo Modena, a gold medal winner in World War I and the son of General Angelo Modena, president of the Supreme Army and Navy Tribunal in the late 1920s. In 1938, Ugo Modena, along with twenty-four other Jewish generals and five admirals, was abruptly dismissed. He refused to apply for an exemption and retired quietly to the country. When his children were forced to leave school, however, he could no longer bear it. He wrote a courteous letter to his king, requesting that, if his medals and service had any meaning, his children be reinstated. The king promised to try, but General Modena obtained no results. Quietly and without publicity, he returned his medals. [36]

Every Italian Jew was affected. Giorgio Bassani, who later wrote *The Garden of the Finzi-Continis,* had to break off his engagement to a Catholic girl. [37] Rita Levi Montalcini, a 1936 graduate from the University of Turin Medical School, had to leave her job at a research institute. She moved her laboratory into her home—and went on to win the Nobel Prize in Physiology or Medicine in 1986. Carlo Modigliani, who had, in his own words, "forgotten completely about being Jewish," was given one hour's notice to resign his teaching position. Also a talented musician and composer, Modigliani had belonged to a Society of Authors since 1915. In 1919, an operetta he had written was performed in Rome. After the racial laws, he received a letter informing him that he was no longer a member of the society. He received no explanation. At about the same time, in accordance with the racial laws, the non-Jewish maid who cared for Modigliani's sick and nearly totally deaf eighty-six-year-old mother had to leave. He could not find a Jewish replacement. After much difficulty, he finally found a Catholic woman who was willing to ignore the law and work for him. In the years that followed, she took many risks and proved to be devoted to her charge.[38]

Enzo Levi, a lawyer from Modena mentioned earlier and, like Modigliani, a proud veteran of World War I, also found many individuals willing to take a chance. Racial decrees limited Levi's law practice to Jewish clients. He recalls, however, that many non-Jewish clients came to him secretly, and lawyer friends often let him use their names. In this respect, Levi was more fortunate than many. In other towns, even Jewish clients were pressured to use non-Jewish professionals.

For Enzo Levi and his wife, the educational constraints were the most painful aspect of the racial laws. The Levis lived near the elementary school, which their younger children could no longer attend. At the close of every day, the grieving youngsters could hear the voices of their friends in the school yard. The older Levi children were also excluded from the secondary school. They could enter it only for state examinations, for which they prepared in their Jewish schools. They took the written portions in a separate room and were always questioned last in the oral examinations. The Levis finally left Italy in 1942. As Enzo Levi wrote in his memoirs, "At least five centuries . . . of life of my family in Italy, my own passionate participation in the war, a lifetime of honest work on my part and on the part of my ancestors . . . were not valid in identifying me as a citizen of my country."[39]

Carlo Modigliani survived for a time by teaching at the newly constituted Jewish School of Milan. Giorgio Bassani, fresh from the university and seeking his first job, did the same in Ferrara. Enzo Levi also solved one problem by sending his older children to the Jewish School in Modena. Before 1938, not even the most religious families sent their children to Jewish secondary schools unless they wanted to become rabbis. After 1938, special schools played a major role in the lives of thousands of teachers, students, and parents.

Fabio Della Seta's Jewish high school in Rome was located near the old ghetto, on the other side of the Tiber River. About 350 middle-class students were thus brought back to the very streets their parents and grandparents, with so much effort, had left behind. Della Seta expected all the students at the Jewish School to be brilliant because, as he says, "it is known that in every class there is a 'first,' and almost always it is a Jew." His image of his people was as stereotyped as that of non-Jews. "What is a Jew?" he asks. "Someone who [in the public schools] does not go to the religious lessons."[40]

Della Seta's experience at the Jewish School changed his life. Not all the students were brilliant, but most of his teachers were. They had recently lost jobs in universities and other secondary schools.[41] For the teachers, it became a point of honor to prepare students to excel on state exams. As a result of the school, Della Seta remembers, "one was no longer ashamed to be Jewish. Even those, and they were perhaps the major part, who came from families with Risorgimento traditions—laic, therefore, with a clear strain of anticlericalism, naturally also anti-Jewish—began to sense a strange, unmotivated pride in being Jewish."[42] Students developed a great interest in Jews who were famous—Einstein, Freud, Spinoza, Kafka. Some even began to attend religious services.

Of course Della Seta's memories are not all positive; he poignantly describes the isolation and despair of the period. As the Holocaust approached, students drew away from their families, where catastrophe was the main subject of conversation. They focused entirely upon themselves, on research and polemics, acting, he says, as if all the world's problems could be solved by mathematics or reduced to a correct reading of Kafka or Dostoevsky. In their bewilderment, helplessness, and isolation, they resemble the characters in Bassani's *Garden of the Finzi-Continis.* [43] Bassani clearly understood the desperate attempt, when one is helpless to influence big events, to pretend that only small ones matter.

Jewish schools also functioned in Trieste, Milan, Venice, Florence, Turin, and other major cities, employing the cream of the recently unemployed Jewish professional classes. They continued heroically until the German occupation. Modigliani describes the last examination period at the Milan Jewish School, in the autumn of 1943. The Germans were already in Milan, and neighbors warned teachers and students assembled at the school that Nazis had come looking for them two days before. Exams on the first day were held in the cellar, with an escape route planned and with teachers and students guarding the main entrance. According to regulations, a government supervisor, in this case a non-Jewish woman, was present. She suggested that, for safety, examinations on the following days be held in her apartment. Upon their conclusion, the school closed its doors, and students and teachers alike spent the next year and a half in hiding. [44]

The Jewish schools and, more generally, the racial laws themselves often had the effect of instilling a new sense of Judaism into a highly assimilated and previously indifferent community. In addition to Della Seta's testimony, we have that of Gastone Orefice, the young man from Livorno. Orefice remembers endless discussions with fellow students on the subject of conversion. Their Jewishness seemed such a remote influence in their lives that a refusal to convert often appeared mere stubbornness. A closer examination of their special heritage helped them appreciate its role and meaning. Without the racial laws, most would never have made such an evaluation.[45]

While Jews were considering, and usually rejecting, conversion, Catholic priests took various positions on the issue. Many were willing to backdate baptismal certificates for the children of mixed marriages to qualify converts for exemption from the racial laws. Others interpreted their role much more broadly, however, and used the possibility of racial persecution as a means of gaining converts. They encouraged false rumors: only Catholics could emigrate to South America; the Vatican soon would be able to protect all Catholics, whether of mixed parentage or not; the government was about to Aryanize all Catholics, regardless of parentage. While Levi rightly condemns such methods, he speaks admiringly of other priests, who refused to sanction conversions under false pretenses. One priest told a friend of Levi's, who believed that conversion would lead to Aryanization and save his wife and children, that the rumor was not true. He refused the conversion, but promised the man a false date on a baptismal certificate if the rumor ever became fact.[46]

The racial laws broke the great popular consensus that Mussolini had created with the Ethiopian War. After 1938, the prime minister's popularity declined each year until the end. While most Italians could accept claims that Zionists were disloyal, that Jewish refugees caused price increases and crowded facilities, or that Leon Blum was a natural enemy of Mussolini, they could not accept persecution of the family next door. Furthermore, with the racial program, average Italians realized more clearly than ever that Fascist laws did not demand unquestioning obedience; they could be and were being broken every day. They saw Fascist notables bend the rules for or against the Jews, depending on circumstances, and they began to do the same.

Carlo Modigliani found a Catholic maid to care, illegally,

47

for his mother. Enzo Levi found supportive colleagues and friendly priests. A young university graduate in Turin named Emanuele Artom could not use the library for research on a book, but he found a former teacher who allowed him to take books home.[47] A young mother in Trieste named Laura Erbsen received phone calls from friendly shopkeepers asking her not to come near their shops. They were ashamed that she would see the signs they had been forced to put in their windows: "No Jews or dogs allowed."[48]

An industrialist named Giuseppe Segre, later deported with his wife to Poland, had to fire two faithful non-Jewish servants —two elderly women, who cried and said they had no place to go, but had to leave nevertheless. The next day, two servants from a family in the same building knocked on Segre's door and asked if they could serve him, naturally without pay.[49]

Such attitudes extended to public officials as well. In 1938, Laura Erbsen received a dreaded knock on the door. Policemen told her they had terrible news. She was terror-stricken. The news, they said, was that she would have to let her maid go. She was immensely relieved, but they were crestfallen and deeply ashamed. "How will you manage? You have a new baby, an elderly mother, and a big house." She assured them that the news could have been worse.

The next news was clearly worse. The Erbsens were expelled from Italy in 1939 because the husband was a foreign Jew. When they left the country, many friends came to the train station to see them off. Among them was the father of Mrs. Erbsen's childhood friend, who was a retired general and an official in the Fascist party section in Trieste. After the train was underway, officials charged with seeing expelled persons across the border began their customs inspection. One inspector knocked on Mrs. Erbsen's compartment door and saw that she was wearing jewelry. Only a small amount of jewelry could be taken out of the country, and she had been told that it was safest to keep it on her person. "Put your baby to sleep," he said, "and I will return. And why don't you change and prepare for your journey?" She understood that he did not want to see the jewelry. He never asked for it.[50]

Many others had similar experiences. Frontier guards allowed illegal Jewish immigration (after 1943, some would allow illegal Jewish emigration to Switzerland). Police searched Enzo Levi's house for an illegal radio, and he had the distinct impression that they did not want to find it.[51] But perhaps the best story is that told by Carlo Modigliani of his eighty-six-year-old, nearly deaf mother. Seeking refuge from Milanese air raids in a small village near Varese in February 1943, she had to register with a local official and declare her religion. "I am of the religion that does no evil to any living soul," she declared. "Well then, you are an Aryan," he replied, and thus she was registered. When the Germans arrived a few months later, she survived because of that registration.[52]

Even the most important Fascist leaders occasionally showed a lack of enthusiasm for the racial laws. Roberto Farinacci, Fascist boss of Cremona and one of the country's most vocal Jew baiters, long resisted firing his Jewish secretary. Later, during the German occupation, he turned a list of fifty-three Jews of Cremona over to the Nazis, who were demanding it, but he first warned the individuals on the list that they should hide.[53] Dino Grandi, former *squadrista*, foreign minister, and ambassador to London, passed Giancarlo Sacerdoti's father in the street in Bologna and, when Sacerdoti delicately tried to ignore him to spare him embarrassment, Grandi greeted him jovially with the words, "Ciao, Sacerdoti, don't you recognize an old friend?"[54] Tullio Tamburini, a vicious Fascist *squadrista* from Florence who became chief of police during the German occupation, wrote a letter of recommendation for an exemption for Memo Bemporad's family, his former employers. Mario Piazzesi, Fascist party secretary in Lucca and

Bemporad's former schoolmate, did the same, loudly telling a crowd waiting near his office, "We will make them hear our voice in Rome: we pure Fascists are not anti-Semites, those are German matters." [55]

There is broader, less personal evidence of popular disapproval of the racial laws within the Fascist party. Between 1938 and 1943, over one thousand Fascists lost membership cards because of "pietism," the name given to the crime of sympathizing with Jews. [56] Plans for university chairs on racial studies never materialized. Local Fascist party sections in the largest cities were instructed to establish Centers for the Study of the Jewish Problem, and by 1942 most had done so. Popular participation, however, was negligible. By the fall of Mussolini in July 1943, only 864 Fascist party members out of a total of over 4,000,000 were enrolled as participants. In Milan alone, of 10,000 Fascist party members, 65 were enrolled. [57]

However, the record is uneven. Bemporad's family ignored the law one summer and took lodgings in a beach hotel where they were well known. The hotel management was willing, but someone complained and they had to leave. [58] Police had not wanted to find Levi's radio, but someone—he suspected a competitor—had reported the radio in the first place. Revenue collectors were accommodating with Laura Erbsen and her jewelry, but other officials mercilessly demanded bribes from desperate refugees trying to leave Trieste. [59] Friendly shopkeepers apologized for their "No Jews allowed" signs, but the existence of such signs in the first place was a national disgrace. Bureaucrats processing exemption applications often deliberately humiliated applicants. Many employers were more zealous in firing Jewish employees than the law required. Businessmen were sometimes eager to grab Jewish property. Non-Jewish Italians were showing symptoms of an already deadly disease.

Perhaps the saddest indictments, however, are those that

must be directed against the Church and the king. Pope Pius XI himself had condemned atheistic Nazi anti-Semitism in the papal encyclical *Mit brennender Sorge* in March 1937, but a year and a half later he offered few objections to the Italian racial laws. His protests and those of Pius XII, who succeeded him in March 1939, primarily concerned the treatment of Jews who had converted. The Church strongly objected to Fascist interference with the sacrament of marriage and to Fascist denials of valid conversions. The Church as an institution objected, in other words, to biological racism, but was less strongly opposed to anti-Semitism.[60]

While most Jews may have expected little from the institutional Church, they expected far too much from the monarchy. Jewish veneration of the House of Savoy cannot be overemphasized. Dating from the Jewish emancipation, it was an irrational and deeply embedded attitude that united individuals who managed to disagree about almost everything else. Nearly every Jewish home, shop, and place of worship had a portrait of King Victor Emmanuel III. Yet when Mussolini, before the racial laws, made discreet inquiries about the king's position, Victor Emmanuel expressed no objections. The laws were issued in his name.[61]

Augusto Segre has written an amusing account of his father's disillusionment with the king. Years earlier, the elder Segre, rabbi of Casale, had come under considerable pressure to include Mussolini's name in the traditional blessing of king and country. As the rabbi did not like Mussolini, he tried for a time to claim forgetfulness. Eventually, however, he had to tack on the prime minister's name at the end of his blessing, followed by some words in Hebrew. His congregation, not understanding Hebrew, was satisfied. After 1938, the rabbi shifted the name of the king from the middle of the blessing to the end, linking it with Mussolini. He repeated the same Hebrew words. Segre leaves us to imagine what those words actually were.[62]

4

The War Years:
June 1940-September 1943

THE MORNING after Mussolini declared war on the Allies, Italian police began to arrest foreign Jews. At first they seized only men between the ages of eighteen and sixty. They held their victims for weeks in major city prisons—places like San Vittore in Milan, Marassi in Genoa, and Regina Coeli in Rome, which were to become dreaded household names in the years to come. Conditions were appalling. Toilet facilities were virtually nonexistent, and overcrowding compounded the filth. Eventually the men, in manacles, were sent by train to wretched internment camps at Ferramonti Tarsia in the province of Cosenza, Campagna in the province of Salerno, and others, usually in remote areas of southern Italy. By September 1940 there were fifteen such camps. At Ferramonti and Campagna, there were already about four hundred prisoners each.[1] Men lived in unfinished huts, without electricity or water. Malaria was endemic.[2]

Although Italy was officially a racist country, the primary purpose of the arrests of foreign Jews was not to persecute them as Jews but to intern them as presumably anti-Axis refugees. For the same reason, police also arrested many enemy nationals living in Italy. Most Italian Jews, on the other hand, were not bothered, unless their political pasts suggested potential anti-Fascism to the increasingly paranoid authorities. By the same token, the poor treatment of foreign Jewish prisoners was not a result of deliberate cruelty or racism. All prisoners were similarly treated in Fascist Italy—with indifference and supreme contempt.

From sheer necessity, the prisoners at Ferramonti organized themselves to provide facilities. They completed the huts and dug wells. Eventually, they did much more. Women and children began to arrive. Left without economic means, some actually joined their men voluntarily. More elaborate facilities were required. Prisoners organized a nursery, library, school, theater, and synagogue. They held concerts and athletic events. They established baths, medical offices, and even a pharmacy. Life became bearable, and the initially harsh attitude of most Fascist guards softened into one of trust and respect.

By 1942, about 1,400 people were interned at Ferramonti. [3] Most were German refugees, with smaller numbers of Czechs, Poles, Hungarians, and Yugoslavians. Most were from the middle classes, for the poor could rarely afford to leave their countries. Those with special skills found work in the camp as artisans, gardeners, cooks. Some became food vendors, wandering about the camp selling pastries or hot tea. The general atmosphere was peaceful but efficient. With neat rows of white huts looking out over barren hills and cultivated fields, Ferramonti reminded one visitor of Israel. [4] Unlike Israeli settlements, however, the Italian camp was surrounded with barbed wire and watchtowers.

The Italians and The Holocaust

Fascist policy was often directed toward breaking up families, as in the case of Arthur Frankel. Frankel had lived in Italy since 1912, becoming a citizen in 1923. The racial laws had revoked his citizenship. On July 19, 1940, he and his family were arrested—police were no longer limiting their arrests to men. Frankel was sent to Cosenza, his wife to Potenza, and two other relatives to Avellino. Their three-year-old daughter was left in Milan.[5]

In addition to internment camps, the government maintained a second system of detention known as enforced residence or confinement, in which individuals or whole families were held under light surveillance in private houses in small villages. Before the war, anti-Fascists convicted of minor offenses had often been held in this way. In *Christ Stopped at Eboli*, Carlo Levi describes his experiences of confinement in the 1930s.[6] For the war years, a Jewish woman from Galicia, whose account bears only the initials K. L., offers a brief description.[7]

Mrs. L. lived in Merano, near Bolzano, with her husband, also a foreigner, and their three-year-old child. They operated a large wholesale textile outlet. Mrs. L.'s ordeal began even before Italy entered the war. In August 1939, the government demanded that all Jews not born in Merano leave that town so near the Austrian frontier. Mrs. L., expecting to be away only a short time, put all her belongings in storage and left with her family for Lake Garda.

On July 6, 1940, at 6 A.M., Mrs. L. and her family were arrested. After many delays, lies, and attempts to separate the parents from their child, Mrs. L. and her child were sent to Trea, in the province of Macerata, and her husband, typically, was sent elsewhere. Perhaps because she became very ill, she was reunited with her husband after several weeks. The family was then sent to Orsogna, in the province of Chieti, where they remained until September 1943.

The War Years: June 1940–September 1943

In Orsogna, Mrs. L. and her family lived in a normal house. They received an allowance of thirteen and a half lire a day, which she says was enough to live on. They also probably received a monthly housing allowance of about fifty lire. While they could move freely around the village, they could not leave it. They were not constantly guarded, but they had to report regularly to the police. They could send and receive mail. Mrs. L.'s was only one of ten Jewish families confined in Orsogna. She says that, at least in her case, the villagers all knew she was Jewish but never troubled her. Also in Orsogna were about fifty non-Jewish families—enemy nationals similarly confined.

The famous Italian Jewish author Natalia Ginzburg, from Turin, also recorded a period of enforced residence. [8] Natalia was the sister of Mario Levi, who escaped to Switzerland at the time of the Ponte Tresa affair in 1934. In 1938, she married Leone Ginzburg, son of a wealthy family from Odessa but raised and educated in Italy. Leone, a young university instructor of Slavic languages, had established his anti-Fascist credentials early in 1934 by refusing to sign the oath of loyalty to the Fascist regime demanded of all professors since 1931. He promptly lost his first job. Soon after, he was arrested for complicity in the Ponte Tresa affair and, with Sion Segre Amar, given a light sentence. A year later, he was arrested and sentenced again for his activities as a leader of Giustizia e Libertà.

Leone Ginzburg became an Italian citizen, but the racial laws revoked that status. In June 1940, as a foreign Jew and a known anti-Fascist, he was arrested again. He was sent to enforced residence in the small town of Pizzoli in the Abruzzi, where Natalia and their two sons were allowed to join him two months later. They remained there together until the fall of Mussolini. Natalia remembers those years as among the best in their tragically brief life together. Leone somehow managed to continue his work as a director of the new Einaudi publishing company. They were able to walk in the countryside beyond the village, and they began to appreciate rural life for the first time. Their third child, a daughter, was born early in the summer of 1943.

After Mussolini's fall in July 1943, Leone Ginzburg returned to Rome to resume political activity with Giustizia e Libertà. It is an indication of his feeling for the village of his enforced residence that he left Natalia and his children there. When the Germans invaded in September, his family joined him in Rome —Natalia simply climbed aboard a German truck, telling the driver they were war refugees and had lost their papers. They all went into hiding, but Leone intensified his Resistance work. He was arrested in November. In February 1944, Natalia learned that he had died mysteriously in the infirmary of Regina Coeli prison. The period of enforced residence became, for her and the children, a memory of enforced tranquillity. [9]

Internment camps for civilians, whether Italian for Jews, British for Boers, or American for Japanese Americans, are in all cases abhorrent. They become even more inexcusable when the interned individuals have demonstrated their loyalty through years of residence, hard work, and, often, citizenship in their adopted country. They become nightmares when internees suffer, as in Italy, from lack of food, shelter, and medicine, and from official neglect and indifference. As bad as the camps were, however, life for Jews there was better than in other countries in occupied Europe. As discussed earlier, about 6,500 of Italy's 10,000 foreign and denationalized Jews had left the country by September 1939—also disgraceful, but nevertheless true. Of the 7,000 foreign Jews known to be in Italy in October 1941, at least 3,000 were new arrivals. [10] It is a tragic index of the times that most refugees were grateful for whatever they found in Italy.

As the war progressed, Italian treatment of Jewish refugees softened, and enforced residence became more common than internment. Enemy nationals joined the Jewish families under surveillance. Nor was enforced residence limited to the harshest southern mountain villages. Refugees were housed throughout northern and central Italy as well. Augusto Segre recalls that in 1942, about four hundred Yugoslavian Jewish refugees lived as enforced residents around Asti in northern Piedmont. He was able to visit and assist them on a regular basis.[11] If those four hundred people had remained in German-occupied zones of Yugoslavia, they would have been deported by the Nazis or murdered by the Croatian terrorists whom the SS allowed to operate with impunity. Italy was one of the few countries to grant them asylum.

Primo Levi, survivor of Auschwitz and prize-winning author today, also remembers a beneficiary of Italian refugee policy. Olga, a young Croatian Jew, fled to Piedmont with her entire family in 1942. While in enforced residence, she learned to speak Italian. She belonged, Levi remarks, "to that flood of thousands of foreign Jews who had found hospitality, and a brief peace, in the paradoxical Italy of those years, officially anti-Semitic."[12] Hospitality is a strange word for enforced residence, but those were strange times. Olga lived gratefully in Italy until the German occupation. Left without protection, she and her family were then deported to Auschwitz. Primo Levi met her there after the liberation. Of her entire family, only she survived.

Finally, it must be noted that until the German occupation, Mussolini's government did not release a single Jew to the Nazis for deportation. The Germans were unable to secure even the German refugees on Italian soil. Dr. Carltheo Zeitschel from the German Embassy in Paris reported after a visit to Rome:

The German Embassy in Rome has for years the strictest orders from Berlin not to do anything that might in any way disturb the friendly relations between Italy and Germany. It is unthinkable, it seems, for the German Embassy in Rome to touch such a burning subject as the Jewish question in Italy. [13]

Also, as will be seen, Italian government officials protected both indigenous and refugee Jews in Italian-occupied territories in Croatia, Greece, and southern France, despite considerable German pressure there. [14] In contrast, the Vichy French authorities agreed to deliver foreign Jews to the Nazis for deportation in July 1942, several months before German armies entered unoccupied France, and actually handed over seven thousand by August. [15] They withdrew the protection that Fascist Italy never denied its refugees.

While Jews in Fascist Italy were free from the danger of deportation, and while conditions were worse in other countries, daily life during the war remained difficult. First of all, arrests, internment camps, and enforced residence were not limited to foreigners. About two hundred Italian Jews were also arrested in the early days of the war, and by 1943, their number had grown to over a thousand. [16] A few victims were charged as anti-Fascists, although most active anti-Fascists had been arrested or had emigrated long ago. Others were described as Socialists, Republicans, former radicals, anarchists, Zionists, Freemasons, defeatists, subversives, or spies. One was described simply as leading a "mysterious life." [17] In fact, these Italian citizens were victims of the paranoid suspicion the racial laws had created. Their coreligionists lived in constant apprehension of similar suspicion and arrest.

In addition, as the war fanned popular emotions, ugly anti-Semitic violence began to occur in Italy. By far the worst cases took place in Trieste, where Jewish shops had been vandalized and signs reading "No Jews allowed" had appeared in store windows even before the war. Germans, Italians, Slavs, and

The War Years: June 1940–September 1943

Jews lived side by side in Trieste and heartily disliked one another. About 4 percent of the population was Jewish—much more than the national average—and Jews played a visible role at the highest levels of society. The city always had a stronger anti-Semitic element than the rest of Italy. Furthermore, Italian tolerance and skepticism of government had never prevailed there. Trieste shared the Austrian tradition of taking laws seriously, and the laws sanctioned anti-Semitism.

After Italy entered the war, attacks on Jewish individuals and shops in Trieste increased significantly. Fascist thugs raided cafés frequented by Jews, beating up anyone they could catch. In October 1941, they assaulted the local synagogue, writing curses on the outer walls and shattering windows. Teachers allegedly let children out of school to participate. On July 18, 1942, a second assault reached inside the synagogue. Vandals destroyed sacred scrolls and books, lamps and furniture. The dates of these incidents are significant because, it must constantly be recalled, the German occupation of Italy did not occur until September 1943. Anti-Semitic violence in Trieste cannot be blamed on the Nazis. [18]

Similar but less frequent incidents occurred in many other Italian cities. In Ferrara, particularly vicious anti-Semitic tracts were distributed to the public in July and September 1940. Then on September 21, 1941, vandals destroyed the synagogue of Ashkenazi rite and beat a rabbi. [19] At about the same time in Turin, anti-Semitic graffiti began to appear on walls, especially in neighborhoods near the synagogue. On the night of October 14, 1941, incendiaries with gasoline tried unsuccessfully to ignite the synagogue itself. Then on October 15, 16, and 17, vicious posters calling for death to Jews, accompanied by long (and according to Emanuele Artom, often inaccurate) lists of local Jewish names and addresses, appeared along Turin's main streets. [20] Artom twice suggested in his diary that German agents may have been responsible for these outrages, but he had no proof. [21] Certainly a brilliant university graduate from a family distinguished for generations of service in Italy would have preferred to believe that outside agitators, not Italians, were the guilty parties.

In fact, foreign provocateurs seem to have played a negligible role in the anti-Semitic violence of the early war years. Many incidents were purely spontaneous, as, for example, the attack on the synagogue in Casale Monferrato, which Augusto Segre witnessed and described as an escapade of Fascist youths who had just viewed an anti-Semitic movie at a local theater. [22] Other acts, such as the synagogue attacks in Trieste and Ferrara, were more carefully planned. They seem, however, to have resulted not from foreign provocateurs or even from Fascist pressure at high levels, but from petty rivalries between local party sections or individuals, all attempting to appear more Fascist than their comrades. [23] Police response to incidents was equally unpredictable. In his own small city, Segre found that the local police chief ignored his complaints and said he could do nothing. On the other hand, the *carabinieri* chief, a friend of his parents, was outraged and provided immediate protection. [24]

Most Italian Jews, however, not directly affected by either the political arrests or the anti-Semitic incidents, probably suffered most during the war from their sense of isolation and irrelevance. Jewish men, of course, could not be drafted for military service, nor could they contribute to military production. Indeed, in one of the most pathetic demonstrations of the absurdity of the racial laws and the depth of Jewish patriotism, some Italian Jews wrote Mussolini, begging to be allowed to fight for their country. They were refused. The government made only one exception, in the case of Umberto Pugliese, inspector general of the Naval Engineer Corps. In 1938, the racial laws had forced General Pugliese into early retirement at the age of fifty-eight. In November 1940, his desperate government summoned him as the man most qualified to raise the fleet sunk by the British at Taranto. When asked what payment he would require, he replied that he wanted nothing more than a round-trip ticket to Taranto and the right to wear his uniform with his decorations during the performance of his duty. General Pugliese completed his assignment and then quietly returned to retirement. [25]

As another example of the absurdity of the racial policy, Augusto Segre tells the story of his cousin, Bruno Jesi. Jesi's father had died from wounds received at the front during World War I. Jesi himself had lost a leg as a result of valiant service in the Ethiopian War. His military record was most impressive. Not only had he saved, at great personal risk, the lives of several wounded men in his unit in Ethiopia, but he had crossed enemy lines on horseback to bring a Catholic military chaplain to attend a dying man. On the insistence of a Catholic cardinal, Bruno Jesi received a gold and a bronze medal in January 1941, with the racial laws in full effect and with Italy at war. He was honored in a fine ceremony at an army base at Turin, in the presence of the highest military, civil, and religious authorities. He received his medals for military valor at a time when no Jews could serve in the armed forces. He died in 1943 from the delayed effect of his wounds. [26]

While many Jews might have liked to serve, many more non-Jews deeply resented the fact that they did not. Ugly accusations began to circulate that Jews were (somehow) getting rich while other boys were dying for their country. Partly to counteract such complaints, a new decree appeared on May 6, 1942. All Italian Jews between the ages of eighteen and fifty-five were required to register for labor service. Even Jews with exemptions were to be included.

Emanuele Artom's experience with forced labor in Turin was probably typical. [27] Presumably, he and his father registered immediately, as required, but they were not summoned until October. At that time, 180 men were called, divided into three equal groups, and assigned to unload wood, work on roads, and handle coal. With his customary humor, Artom describes a convert, apparently not recognized as such by the Fascists, whom the other Jews scrupulously avoided. He also remembers a man who protested that he had not been called and insisted upon enlisting immediately as a volunteer. Artom and his highly educated middle-class friends debated the possibility of formally requesting the larger bread, pasta, and rice rations to which factory workers (but not Jewish forced laborers) were entitled. The Fascists would undoubtedly not have enjoyed the joke.

The actual work was long and hard. Those in Artom's group were not accustomed to manual labor. They could not rest, drink, or smoke while working. They received only a token hourly wage. They had to wear workmen's overalls. Many victims of the forced-labor program allege that primarily middle-class Jews were called, in a deliberate effort to harass and humiliate them. Artom makes no such suggestion, but he was vividly aware of the dramatic role reversal between workers and supervisors. "I was a street cleaner," said one supervisor to Artom, "and I have passed from the street to the office." "We, instead," Artom replied, "have passed from the office to the street." After a day's hard labor, the Jews, anxious to return to their libraries or their offices, would say, "See you later. We are going to work." The guards would reply, "We, instead, are going home."[28]

Not all those eligible for forced labor were called. Women were usually not called, and the work itself rarely lasted more than a few weeks. There were exceptions, however. Artom heard that in nearby Alessandria, notorious until liberation for its fanatic Fascist section, everyone was called—men and women alike. Medical exemptions, however, could be requested in all cities. In Turin, at least, municipal officials and doctors considered these requests with elaborate attention, courtesy, and surprising concurrence.

Other personal accounts of forced-labor service generally resemble Artom's. During the autumn of 1942, Marcello Morpurgo of Gorizia worked for a time in a sawmill. He realized that the owner needed workers and had applied to the new forced labor program for them. Like Artom, Morpurgo approached the situation with an ironic sense of humor. For his first meeting with the sawmill owner, he dressed in his best suit and presented his calling card. The confused owner called Fascist headquarters, complaining that he wanted workers, not university graduates.

Work at the sawmill was hard, and Morpurgo was not a skilled laborer. He says he deliberately worked badly and wasted wood, as his little contribution to the war effort. He was soon transferred to a factory that made tiles. There he did light work in the morning, ran errands, and tutored the owner's children in the afternoon. The owner and his family were kind to him. Morpurgo also reports that medical exemptions were easy to obtain and doctors were very understanding, particularly after the first weeks when Fascists turned their attention elsewhere. Like so many Fascist endeavors, he says, the forced-labor program finally just petered out. It never ended by actual decree. [29]

In Ferrara in September 1942, Gianni Ravenna was required to load heavy boxes of fruit. Jewish women worked also, sorting the fruit. Ravenna confirms that the program slowly fell apart, but he provides an interesting twist. Many people in Ferrara, he claims, did not approve of the racial laws and regarded the forced-labor program with extreme distaste. Jews in the program began to be regarded with more favor than ever—a reason, perhaps, for ending it. [30]

Actual statistics on the forced-labor program confirm that,

in most areas, it was not executed with vigor. On July 31, 1943, a few days after the fall of Mussolini, an official report declared that 15,517 people had registered for labor. Of these, 2,410 had received temporary exemptions and 1,301, permanent ones. Of the remaining 11,806 people, 2,038 had actually worked—only 13 percent of the total registered. [31]

For most Italian Jews during the war, life simply went on, a little harder and a little sadder than before. Everyone knew families with members who had converted, emigrated, or been arrested. Many endured unpleasant anti-Semitic incidents and noticed that certain Christian friends no longer recognized them. But as the war continued and grew increasingly unpopular, Augusto Segre, among others, noticed that other old friends made a point of being seen with him. Segre's friend, a soldier home on leave, deliberately and publicly walked with him while in uniform. [32] Such an act in Germany would have put the friend in prison.

With the restrictions of the racial laws, jobs were hard to find. Carlo Modigliani eked out a living teaching at the Jewish School in Milan. When British bombing raids drove many Milanese to the country, he added to his earnings by private tutoring, and not only in Jewish families. He reached his pupils by train, by bicycle, and often on foot. [33] Augusto Segre's job was similarly extra-legal. A university graduate, he worked in the office of a small winery near Asti. His employers wore black shirts faithfully on all public occasions. Privately, they disliked the war and the racial laws. They were perfectly aware that Segre was Jewish. Most of the Piedmontese peasants Segre met at work had never known a Jew before, just as he had scarcely known a peasant. When the Germans arrived, these new friends saved his life. [34]

In addition to the difficult task of earning a living, many Jews became involved with charitable service agencies. Segre worked with an organization that recruited, trained, and supplied documents to young people wishing to emigrate to Palestine. [35] Others devoted themselves to education. Some of the most extensive relief work, however, was directed toward foreign refugees in Italy. That work was largely conducted by the Delegazione Assistenza Emigranti Ebrei, or Delasem, a most remarkable Jewish service agency for an officially anti-Jewish state.

Dante Almansi, newly designated president of the Union of Italian Jewish Communities, was the single individual most responsible for securing government permission for the founding of Delasem in 1939. It will be recalled that Almansi had been, until the racial laws, a Fascist party member and vice-chief of police. He was well connected. In 1939, he called upon former friends and acquaintances to convince them that an agency like Delasem was in Italy's best interests. It would, he argued convincingly, not only relieve the government of the onerous task of caring for unwanted refugees, but would also bring in much-needed foreign exchange. Delasem amply fulfilled both promises.

In the months before the Italian entry into the war, Delasem helped about 2,000 Jewish refugees emigrate abroad, spending about eight million lire on their behalf. During the same period, before the wartime policy of internment, Delasem also provided food, clothing, medicine, and living allowances to about 9,000 other refugees, spending another three and a half million lire. A Delasem report in July 1940 stated that about two and a half million lire came from the contributions of Italian Jews, and the balance—roughly nine million lire—came from abroad. The American Joint Distribution Committee provided about $15,000 a month for assistance programs, and the Hias-Ica Emigration Association (HICEM) supplied funds for emigrants. The Italian government must have been pleased.

The Italians and The Holocaust

After Italy entered the war, Jewish emigration became more difficult, but not impossible. Special trains and planes carried Jews to Spain and Portugal, and, with the tacit consent of the police, special guides conducted them across the frontier into Vichy France. Another 3,000 people managed to leave by the time of the armistice. Of the total of 5,000 Delasem emigrants, about 2,000 went to Spain and Portugal, 800 to North America, 600 to Shanghai, 500 to Tangiers, 400 to France and England, and smaller numbers to Argentina, Cuba, Paraguay, and Palestine. [36]

Delasem also continued to assist thousands of refugees in Italy during the war. Many of these were interned, but Delasem tried, among other things, to encourage enforced residence instead—often to the point of actually providing living quarters. Delasem workers supplied refugees with vital food, clothing, and medicine, and, whenever possible, with books, religious materials, and gifts for children. They tried to reach Jews in every remote area, helping them to locate and communicate with relatives and friends. [37] Funds continued to arrive from the American Joint Distribution Committee by way of Switzerland, and Delasem managed to function with ever-increasing difficulty even during the German occupation.

Young Mario Finzi may well be representative of the quality and dedication of Delasem workers. Finzi was the only child of two secondary school teachers in Bologna. He was just beginning to practice law in Milan when the racial laws ended his career. A highly talented musician, he moved to Paris to attempt a new career as a pianist. High praise from his teacher, invitations to give concerts, and a French radio contract all indicated future success in his new endeavor. In August 1939, however, he returned to Italy to renew his visa and could not leave. The Germans had invaded Poland. Mario Finzi began to teach in Bologna's Jewish School, and became involved with refugees. In 1940, he became the Delasem representative in his native city.

Arrested in Bologna by the Fascist government early in 1943, Finzi remained in prison until Badoglio freed him. After the German occupation of Italy, he continued his work, helping Italian Jews in hiding as well as foreigners. Giancarlo Sacerdoti, one of his students, recalls that he never carried a gun, feeling that it would be wrong to shoot another human being. In March 1944, Mario Finzi was recognized during a routine document check in his home city. He was arrested and deported to Auschwitz. There, according to Sacerdoti, unwilling to brutalize his sensibilities in order to survive, he threw himself on the high-tension wire that surrounded the camp. He left a message for his parents, begging their forgiveness. He was thirty-one. [38]

The story of the children of Villa Emma stands out as Delasem's finest achievement. [39] The spectacular rescue effort began with Lelio Vittorio Valobra, a lawyer from Genoa, vice-president of the Union of Italian Jewish Communities, and national director of Delasem. In the spring of 1942, Valobra learned from Eugenio Bolaffio, his Delasem representative in Gorizia, that a number of children had survived the terrible massacres of Jews in German-occupied parts of Yugoslavia and were hiding in the countryside around Ljubljana. He traveled to Ljubljana, then in the Italian-occupied zone. There he learned that a large group had sought refuge in a castle in no man's land, in an area overrun by partisans and not clearly occupied by either Italians or Germans. With the help of a woman who was president of the Slovenian Red Cross, Valobra obtained a car and reached the castle. He found forty-two Jewish children between the ages of nine and twenty-one. Some were Yugoslavian, but most were refugees from Germany, Poland, Rumania, and Austria. Their parents had been murdered.

Somehow Valobra managed to transport the children to safety in Ljubljana, where they stayed for a few months. During that period, he secured permission from his officially anti-Semitic government to move them into Italy. In the little village of Nonantola, about ten kilometers from Modena, the president of the local Jewish community found a suitable nine-teenth-century villa called Villa Emma. Spared the agonies of internment, the children were installed there as enforced residents. The community doubled in size when about fifty more children between the ages of four and twenty-two arrived, mostly from Croatia, in March and April 1943.

Delasem workers and ordinary Modenese residents took responsibility for the support, education, and supervision of the children. School-aged children studied academic subjects, agriculture, carpentry, and tailoring. A local peasant family named Leonardi taught farm methods to children who would later apply their skills in Israel. A town doctor named Giuseppe Moreali provided free medical care. Another neighbor named Aristide Barani helped with provisioning, and took two of the smallest children into his own home. The local rabbi from Modena celebrated seven marriages.

The already remarkable story of Villa Emma became little short of miraculous after the arrival of the Germans. Shortly after the occupation began, Nazis led by a local Fascist fanatic approached the villa. It was completely empty. Approximately ninety-two children had simply disappeared. Within twenty-four hours, before most Italians were even aware of the Nazi danger, they had found shelter with local residents. They remained in hiding until liberation. Not one was ever caught.

The story of the survival of the Villa Emma children involved a whole cross section of provincial Modenese society: many children were taken in by priests at the local seminary at Nonantola; others went into the homes of local peasants; sharecroppers at one estate took about fifteen; agricultural day laborers took others into their poor homes; artisans like the carpenter Erio Tosatti took still others. In addition to homes, all the children had to have false documents. Dr. Moreali and two priests from the seminary helped solve this problem. They located an old artisan named Primo Apparuti, who made a false seal out of gratitude to a Jew who had once been kind to him. They obtained blank forms from several sources: a sympathetic communal employee in Nonantola, friends at Modena's military academy, a municipal functionary who sold them in exchange for clothes from the Delasem stocks.

Dr. Moreali, the two priests, and all who provided shelter, food, or documents for Jews, risked their lives daily. If caught and found guilty, rescuers were occasionally shot on the spot. If not executed, they were usually deported to German concentration camps, where many died from starvation, disease, hard labor, and the sadism of their guards.[40]

Similar events were occurring all over Italy. The ratio was the same everywhere: A handful of Fascist fanatics, like the one who led the Germans to Villa Emma and the others who arrested local priests and tried unsuccessfully to make them talk, were countered by hundreds who took in Jews, assisted them, or, at the very least, knew exactly where they were and kept quiet. But nowhere else in Italy were the results so spectacular. The problem of disguising ninety-two orphans,none of whom spoke flawless Italian or were familiar with Catholic ritual (essential to those hiding in the seminary), must have seemed insuperable. And yet, somehow, it was done. At least two adults involved in the story—Eugenio Bolaffio, Delasem representative in Gorizia, and Mario Finzi, Delasem representative for Emilia with jurisdiction in Nonantola—disappeared in the death camps, but all the children survived.

By the summer of 1943, Italy's independent war effort was clearly drawing to a close. On July 10, U.S. and British troops landed in Sicily, and the race for Messina began. Sicilian villagers welcomed them loudly, trampling pictures of Mussolini in the dust. On July 19, when the Allies bombed Rome for the first time, thousands who had believed the Holy City to be immune from air attack felt the fear that had become common in northern cities. A local Fascist club asked Romans for contributions to aid the bombing victims. A friend of Fabio Della Seta from the Jewish School gave some linens, and when thanked, told them he was Jewish. No one cared. [41]

At 10:45 P.M. on the hot night of July 25, 1943, Luciano Morpurgo, a Jewish author and editor prohibited by the racial laws from publishing or working, was sitting on the balcony of his apartment in Rome. He was drinking wine with a neighbor and watching the stars in the clear sky. From the streets below, he began to hear shouting and laughing. Are the people always happy, he wondered, even in these terrible times? Then cries of *"Evviva* Badoglio!" began to pierce the night air. He ran to his forbidden radio and heard the great news. [42] Mussolini had been removed. Badoglio was the new prime minister. Fascist leaders were in hiding; it was now their turn to be hunted. Badoglio announced that the war would continue, but no one noticed. Italy was in an uproar.

The next day, joyous crowds assembled everywhere. They broke windows at Fascist party headquarters. They marched on prisons in Rome and Turin, releasing political prisoners. Morpurgo noted in his diary:

> On all the public buildings, swarms of workers removed the Fascist symbols; those of plaster fell quickly, those of marble and traver-

tine had to be chiseled with difficulty. Through the streets passed flocks of boys . . . who with the same mouths that once had shouted "Duce, Duce!" were now shouting . . . "Death to Mussolini, Viva Badoglio." [43]

While most Italians celebrated, Morpurgo was among the few who understood what was coming. He quietly prepared a secret room, a hiding place, just in case.

In the days that followed, the Fascist party was dissolved, the militia was incorporated into the army, and some Fascist leaders were arrested. The Jews, jubilant at the new developments, waited for the racial laws to end. On July 27, Antonio Le Pera, director of the infamous Office of Demography and Race which had rigorously enforced the racial laws, was arrested and placed in a prison cell recently vacated by anti-Fascists freed from Regina Coeli. Telesio Interlandi, the virulently anti-Semitic newspaper editor, was also arrested. These seemed like good signs.

And yet, during his forty-five-day regime, Badoglio did almost nothing more for the Jews. After the war, he explained that an abrogation of the racial laws had been impossible—it would have resulted in violent German opposition. Badoglio not only retained the racial laws, however. He failed even to send a circular to his prefects suggesting that they ease enforcement. He did not officially end forced labor. He did not dissolve the Office of Demography and Race. With regard to the thousands of Italian and foreign Jews in prisons, internment camps, and enforced residence, he sent out a series of vague orders sanctioning the release of those not accused of political activities and those accused of mere anti-fascism. Communists, anarchists, and spies were to be held. In fact, the guidelines were imprecise and confusing. Many Jews, like Leone Ginzburg and Mario Finzi, were released, but most recent refugees remained confined. [44]

The Italians and The Holocaust

Even more serious in the long run, Badoglio took almost no measures to safeguard Jews from the possibility of a German invasion. In this regard, the Jews were not unique, for Badoglio took almost no measures to protect anyone except the king and himself. The consequences of his neglect, however, were particularly disasterous for the Jews. Despite appeals by Jewish leaders and others, Badoglio's bureaucrats refused to destroy their many lists of Jewish names and addresses. Nearly all these lists fell into German hands after September 8.

Badoglio also did nothing to warn Jews in the Italian colonies of Rhodes and Cos and in Italian-occupied Corfu of any impending danger. [45] Hiding places were not easy to secure on the islands, and the occupying Nazis rounded up and deported thousands. [46] The new prime minister did somewhat better in two cases. After considerable pressure from military and diplomatic officers, he issued instructions prohibiting the release of interned Jews to the Croats and, later, allowing Jews in Italian-occupied France to follow the retreating army into Italy. In the days just before the armistice, he also promised to help Jews in France emigrate to North Africa. The fact that Badoglio's promise came too late to save lives was only partially his fault. [47]

Despite any real change in Italy's racial policy, however, most Jews during the Badoglio period sensed that things were improving. Emanuele Artom wrote in his diary on August 7, 1943, "The other day the *Gazzetta del Popolo* [of Turin] cited the honesty of the [Jewish] Minister Luzzatti as exemplary; today his monument has been restored and on the radio the works of Jews are again presented." [48] On September 3, five days before the German occupation that would ultimately destroy his life, he noted that Jews could again publish funeral notices, hire non-Jewish domestics, go to summer resort areas, and have radios. [49] Like most Italians, Jewish and non-Jewish alike, Artom assumed that Badoglio would soon end the war, and he was willing to wait patiently until then for the end of the racial laws.

In fact, for Jews and non-Jews alike, Badoglio's forty-five days constituted a period of unwarranted hope that blinded them to a fearful reality. Very few thought about the six German divisions with one hundred thousand soldiers already in Italy in July, or about the additional troops that had poured in by September, bringing the total to at least eighteen divisions.[50] During the same period, the seven effective Italian divisions in the country did not increase. And very few noticed the unemployed Fascists, bitter, desperate, and ignored. Nursing their grievances, hard-core Fascists were becoming far more fanatical than in their days of glory. Searching for scapegoats, they were becoming more anti-Semitic than ever. Like the Germans, the Jews, and all Italians, they were simply biding their time.

5

Italians and Jews
in the Occupied
Territories

I N HIS MEMOIRS, Primo Levi recalled Olga, the Yugoslavian Jewish refugee who found temporary peace in "paradoxical Italy, officially anti-Semitic." [1] He did not exaggerate. Wartime Italy was indeed a paradox. Italian Jews could be arrested for no apparent cause in their own country, while their government did everything in its power to protect them in German-occupied areas. Italian Jewish doctors, lawyers, and teachers could not practice and were forced to perform manual labor, yet foreign Jewish refugees received rudimentary shelter and living allowances from the same government. Synagogues were sacked with impunity, while Jewish relief agencies were allowed to collect funds abroad and aid refugees.

Nothing demonstrates the paradox more clearly than the exceptional measures of the Italian army, Foreign Ministry, and entire diplomatic corps to protect all Jews in Italian-occupied territories. Italy occupied much of Greece in 1941, part of Croatia at about the same time, and eight departments in southern France in November 1942. In all three areas, military and diplomatic personnel, often without instructions or coordination, acted similarly. They resorted to every imaginable scheme and subterfuge to resist repeated German demands for the deportation of Jews. They ignored Mussolini's directives, occasionally with his tacit consent. They neglected to pass on instructions, made orders deliberately vague and imprecise, invented absurd bureaucratic excuses, lied, and totally misled the Germans. If the subject had not been so serious and the stakes so desperately high, the story might have acquired the dimensions of a comic opera, with befuddled Germans concluding, as usual, that Italians were blatant liars and hopelessly incompetent administrators. But thousands of lives were at stake, and the game was stark and deadly.

The game was also unique, for the behavior of the players bore little resemblance to activities in other nations. In most European countries, but especially in Denmark and in Italy itself somewhat later, individuals tried to save local Jews who were their friends, neighbors, and compatriots. Even in areas friendly to Nazi Germany such as Vichy France, Bulgaria, and Rumania, local authorities resisted German demands for the deportation of native Jews. But they rarely extended their protection to foreign Jews. In complete contrast, the occupying forces in the Italian-controlled territories of Croatia, Greece, and southern France protected total strangers—neither Italian citizens nor, in many cases, even citizens of the occupied country. The only link between protector and victim was their common humanity.

Chronologically, the story of the Italian rescue of foreign Jews begins in Croatia. After a military resistance of eleven days, the kingdom of Yugoslavia capitulated on April 17, 1941, to the invading German army and its Italian, Bulgarian, and Hungarian allies. The Germans immediately occupied Serbia, with its capital at Belgrade, and the Italians seized most of the Dalmatian coast. In Croatia, a nominally independent government was established at Zagreb under the leadership of Ante Pavelíc, chief of the Ustasha, or Croatian Fascist party. Because Pavelíc had close ties with Italian Fascists, Croatia was expected to remain within the Italian sphere of influence. In fact, independent Croatia was almost immediately divided into an Italian and a German military occupation zone, to last for the duration of the war.

During the terrible summer of 1941, Ustasha assassins ran wild in Croatia, destroying entire villages and murdering thousands of Jews and Serbs. Italian policy toward Jews began in response to this rampage. While the Germans tended to give the Ustasha free rein in their zone, individual Italian soldiers refused to look the other way. Without instructions from above, they simply gathered up Jews in military trucks, cars, and even tanks, and moved them to protected areas. Their officers, soon aware of events, did nothing to interfere. Many lives were saved, and the infuriated Ustasha ceased operations in most of the Italian zone. Meanwhile, word spread, and thousands of other Jews and Serbs fled from German to Italian territory. [2]

Julia Hirschl, a Croatian Jew, and her Viennese husband were among the many refugees who came under Italian protection. Desperately fleeing Croatian terrorists, the Hirschls found themselves in a burned-out village in Herzegovina, 1,100 meters above sea level, in the middle of a battle between the Ustasha and Tito's partisans. "Fortunately the Italians arrived," she recalls, "naturally to help the Ustasha, but at the same time they helped us refugees." The Italians protected them and helped them reach Kupari, near Dubrovnik, in the Italian zone. [3]

Of a prewar total of about thirty thousand Jews in Croatia, only a few thousand remained alive in 1942. These survivors faced a new threat that summer, when Ante Pavelić agreed to restrain his Ustasha terrorists and allow the Germans to deport the Jews instead. The Croatian leader even promised to pay thirty marks for every Jew deported. This grisly deal had one serious drawback, however, for three to five thousand Jews had taken refuge in the Italian zone, where the authorities refused to give them up. Croatian and German officials were more than a little embarrassed. Italian occupying forces were playing the role of noble savior, amid much popular approval.

For the first time in the history of Nazi-Fascist relations, the Germans began to interfere with Italian policy toward the Jews. They had not pressed for anti-Semitic measures in Italy itself, but now, in Croatia in 1942, they did. Italians at all levels of command refused to budge. Finally in August 1942, the frustrated Germans appealed to Mussolini himself. The obliging prime minister replied that he had no objections to the deportations. He communicated this position to the Army General Staff clearly, but without detailed instructions or a timetable. Nothing happened.

The Italian response to Mussolini's communication was masterful. Foreign Ministry officials concerned with Croatia met and decided to ignore it. They made careful arrangements with army liaison officers to delay and obfuscate matters as much as possible. Bureaucratic reports began to flow, explaining that while military authorities would hand over some Jews as soon as possible, the matter was immensely complicated.

Croatian Jews subject to deportation had to be separated from foreign Jews who were exempt. Criteria needed to be established. Was place of birth to be the defining characteristic of a Croatian Jew, or should place of residence, citizenship, and family connections be considered? The army needed time.

Such evasion was not easy. With Croatians and Germans constantly complaining, most high-level Italian officials were anxious to avoid personal responsibility for the delay. A reputation as a "pietist," after all, was not good for one's career. Furthermore, military and diplomatic officers wanted to prevent the involvement of Ministry of the Interior personnel, notoriously less sympathetic to Jews than themselves. In October, the Italian Army General Staff finally decided that some concrete action was needed.

Without warning and within a very few days, soldiers rounded up about three thousand Jews in the Italian zone, settled them in a confined area, and began a census.[4] The roundup was traumatic for the victims, who were certain that they were about to be delivered to the Nazis. Tragically, there were even a few suicides. The roundup also prompted a furious response from many Italian army officers who similarly misunderstood the policy. Everyone soon realized, however, that the roundup and census were simply another ruse. The Italians could now show the Germans they were trying, and the Germans could no longer argue that the Jews constituted a security risk.

Diplomatic pressure did not cease with the roundup. After many less formal appeals, Foreign Minister Joachim von Ribbentrop himself met with Mussolini in Rome in late February 1943. The prime minister again agreed to deliver the Croatian Jews. When he conveyed that decision to General Mario Robotti, commander of the Second Army in Yugoslavia, however, Robotti protested strongly. Mussolini's response, confirmed by several sources, is classic. "O.K., O.K.," he is reported to have told Robotti, "I was forced to give my consent to the extradition, but you can produce all the excuses you want so that not even one Jew will be extradited. Say that we simply have no boats available to transport them by sea and that by land there is no possibility of doing so."[5]

As the spring and early summer of 1943 passed, the Italian problem became less one of German diplomatic pressure than one of the physical inability to protect Jews in Croatia. An Allied invasion of Italy itself seemed imminent, involving the probability that many Italian troops based in Yugoslavia would be withdrawn for defense of the homeland. Foreseeing disaster, Italian authorities again did everything in their power to save the Jews in their zone. By July 1943, roughly three thousand people had been transferred to the Island of Arbe in the Gulf of Carnero, just a few miles from the Italian mainland. After the fall of Mussolini on July 25, the Foreign Ministry repeatedly instructed the General Staff that the Jews on Arbe should not be released unless they themselves requested it. The same ministry also began desperate negotiations with other Italian agencies to arrange for the transfer of the Jews to Italy itself.

Fortunately, because Jews in Italy were soon to be hunted and deported also, those negotiations proceeded too slowly. On September 8, 1943, General Eisenhower announced the armistice, and the Italian army in Yugoslavia laid down its arms. In the resulting confusion, all but 204 mostly sick or elderly Jews on Arbe were able to go into hiding or join Tito's partisans before the Germans occupied the island. The 204 were immediately deported to Auschwitz. Roughly 275 of those who joined the partisans also died before liberation. The rest survived—roughly 2,200 out of 2,661 according to one set of figures; about 3,000 out of 3,500 according to another. The numbers are not high relative to other Holocaust statistics. Perhaps for that very reason, the exceptional effort of Italian officials to protect so few Jewish refugees in their Croatian zone of occupation was indeed impressive. [6]

Julia Hirschl and her husband were among the Jews transferred to Arbe. She relates that after the armistice, partisans helped her move to the island of Lissa. From there, a British convoy took her and many others to a huge refugee complex in the Sinai. Twelve hours after she left Arbe, the Germans arrived there and deported all remaining Jews—the men, women, and children the Italians had been protecting for so long. [7]

On his long journey home from Auschwitz after liberation, Primo Levi traveled for a time with a Greek Jewish survivor. They spent two nights at a monastery in Cracow that was sheltering Italian soldiers who had been in Greece and had been captured by the Germans at the time of the armistice. Levi remembers:

> They spoke Greek, some of them with ease, these veterans of the most compassionate military occupation that history records; they talked of places and events with colorful sympathy, in a chivalrous tacit recognition of the desperate valor of the invaded country. [8]

Levi sensed something special in these former occupying forces, but he could not have learned of the finest chapter in their story until later. He could not have known that, like their colleagues in Croatia, they had helped thousands of Jews who were total strangers to them.

Like Yugoslavia, a defeated Greece had been divided into occupation zones in the spring of 1941. Bulgaria received most of Thrace. Germany controlled Crete, Macedonia, a narrow strip of Thrace bordering Turkey, and the city of Salonika with its 53,000 Jews. Italy occupied what remained: the Ionic islands and much of the Greek peninsula, including Athens. The

German zone contained a total of 55,000 Jews. The much larger Italian zone had only 13,000.[9]

The brutal Nazi roundup and deportation of the Jews of Salonika began early in 1943. At that time, officers of the German General Staff invited the Italian General Staff to follow the Nazi example. The Italians not only refused, but insisted that the Germans spare all Jews of Italian origin. In a brief comic scene in an otherwise tragic setting, Italian consulate officials in Salonika then proceeded to define "Italianness" in the broadest possible way. They issued naturalization papers to Jews married to Greeks in the Italian zone and to their children—"minors" often as old as thirty. Any remote relationship to an Italian was sufficient, as was an Italian-sounding name. Indeed, they often demanded no pretext at all.[10] All this was done by representatives of the same government that, at home, had revoked the citizenship of Jews who had lived in Italy for years and had been nationalized as long ago as 1919!

During the Salonika roundups, Italian consulate officials presented the Nazis with daily lists of newly naturalized Italian subjects being detained awaiting deportation. In most cases, detainees were promptly released. Furthermore, scores of Italian soldiers went to detention areas each day to insist that particular female detainees were their wives. These, too, were often released.[11] The Nazis were undoubtedly not fooled. Perhaps they already assumed they would soon reach into Italian-occupied Greece as well. In any case, they were obliging. Italian military trains carried the released Jews to Athens, where they were fed, sheltered, and protected.

Their respite was short. Unlike the Jews in Italian-occupied Croatia, most Greek Jews did not survive. When the Germans occupied all of Greece after the Italian armistice, brutal manhunts began immediately. Nearly half of the 3,500 Jews in Athens were deported in 1944. Over 5,000 from the remaining Greek mainland, and several thousand from Rhodes, Corfu, and Crete soon joined them.[12] The Italians who had protected them until the armistice were gone. There was no one to help.

In France, the story of the Jews and the Italian occupation began about a year and a half later than in Croatia and Greece. Vichy France before occupation was, like Croatia and Italy, an anti-Semitic state. French Jews could not hold public office, teach, or participate in banking, real estate, or military service. Their share in the professions was restricted by quota. Their properties and businesses were subject to expropriation by the General Commissariat of Jewish Affairs.

Foreign Jews in Vichy France fared even worse. Before the occupation, thousands of refugees, mostly from Germany and Austria, were interned in abominable concentration camps where many died. On July 2, 1942, a full four months before the German and Italian occupying forces arrived, Vichy authorities agreed to deliver foreign Jews to the Germans for deportation. Police were to conduct roundups, with the understanding that French Jews would be spared. By the end of August at least seven thousand people had been delivered to the Germans, including, after Prime Minister Pierre Laval's pious insistence in July that families remain united, children under sixteen.[13]

On November 11, 1942, shortly after the Allied landings in Morocco and Algeria, the German army moved into southern France. The Italians, in turn, occupied eight French departments east of the Rhône. Technically, as in "independent" Croatia, the indigenous government remained in place, but in fact, occupying forces controlled events. In the German zone, the French police were encouraged to continue their manhunts for foreign Jews, while the Nazis watched. In the Italian zone, arrests ceased, and Jews already captured but not yet deported were released. Jews actually found themselves better off than before the Italian occupation.

The first direct confrontation between Italian occupation authorities and Vichy administrators occurred in December. The prefect of Alpes-Maritimes, a close friend of Vichy chief of state Henri Philippe Pétain and an ardent collaborator, ordered that all foreign Jews in his department be sent for security reasons to enforced residence in the departments of Drôme and Ardèche. Drôme was partially occupied by the Germans, and Ardèche, west of the Rhône, was entirely in the German zone. Jews sent there would certainly be deported. Italian Foreign Ministry officials immediately canceled the order, explaining that non-French Jews including Italians, of whom there were comparatively few, were under Italian, not French, jurisdiction. By implication, the Vichy administrators could do what they liked with French Jews, but they could not touch the foreigners. [14]

Laval immediately protested. He could understand, he said, why the Italians might want to protect Italian Jews, but why were they concerned about foreigners? [15] Why, indeed, he might have added, after having interned foreign Jews at home? The Italians, however, had placed Laval in an untenable position. He had promised to protect French Jews; how could he arrest them while allowing foreign Jews to go free? As in Croatia, but even more so in a nation with stronger pro-Jewish sympathies, native authorities did not wish to place the Italians in the role of noble savior. The Italian action, soon extended to all eight occupied departments, in effect protected French and foreign Jews alike.

In the weeks that followed, Italian occupying forces prevented other anti-Jewish measures. They refused to allow foreign labor camps in their occupation zone. They forbade the stamping of identification papers or ration books with the word "Jew," as required by a recent French law. In March, they

ordered the French government to annul all arrests and intern-
ments of Jews in their zone, including French Jews. French
police had arrested well over a hundred Jews in February and
were holding them for deportation. In Grenoble and Annecy,
Italian soldiers actually surrounded the prisons where they were
being held to insure their release.

As in Croatia and Greece, reports of Italian policies toward
the Jews spread rapidly, and thousands of refugees fled into the
Italian zone. According to a German report, an area that before
the war had contained 15,000 to 20,000 Jews held 50,000 in
July 1943. [16] Of these, 20,000 to 30,000 were foreigners. Most
refugees gravitated to Nice, where they received the necessary
residence permits and ration cards. From Nice, many were sent
to enforced residence in villages in the interior.

Enforced residence was not necessarily unpleasant. Refugees
were sent to villages in all the Italian-occupied departments,
but the largest numbers went to lovely resort areas where hotel
space and vacation homes were available because of the war.
The most frequently mentioned villages include Mégève,
Saint-Gervais, Chambéry, Vence, Saint-Martin-Vésubie, and
Barcelonnette, which all had the added advantage of being
near the Swiss and Italian frontiers, "just in case." Refugees in
enforced residence had to report to the Italian authorities twice
a day, observe a 9:00 P.M. curfew, and remain within the limits
of their village. Social contacts were not limited, and they were
free to visit restaurants and cafés and organize schools, cultural
centers, and clubs.

For Jews who had been eluding the Nazis for years, enforced
residence in the Italian zone seemed almost like freedom. Before the winter of 1942–43, the young refugee Alfred Feldman,
who lives today in Washington, had spent many months hiding
in Vichy France. His mother and sister had been caught and
deported. His father had escaped from a French labor camp for

foreign Jews and had eventually been sent to Saint-Martin-Vésubie. His son joined him there. Alfred Feldman remembers:

> I arrived at Saint-Martin toward evening and I saw something that I had not been accustomed to seeing for a long time; Jews were passing peacefully through the streets, sitting in the cafés, speaking in French, German, some even in Yiddish. I also saw some *carabinieri* who passed through the narrow streets of the town with their characteristic Napoleonic hats, and even a group of *bersaglieri* [Italian elite light infantry] with their black plumes. Everything seemed to be happening freely, there were no particular regulations concerning relations between refugees. Discussion flourished with the greatest liberty. [17]

Another survivor recalled Saint-Martin years later, and mused, "All in all, the people were not unhappy, and it would have been beautiful if that state of things could have lasted until the end of the war, but it was too beautiful to last." [18]

Needless to say, Italian protection of the Jews in their zone enraged the Nazis, and the German Foreign Ministry exerted considerable pressure for the delivery of refugees for deportation. Foreign Minister Joachim von Ribbentrop added the issue to his discussion of Croatian Jews when he met Mussolini in Rome in late February 1943. Hans Georg von Mackensen, German ambassador to Italy, also had at least two conversations with the prime minister on the subject. As with the Croatians, Mussolini apparently told the Germans everything they wanted to hear. In a telegram on March 18, 1943, Mackensen reported that Mussolini had said:

> This is a question with which the [Italian] Generals must not meddle. Their attitude is the result not only of lack of understanding, but also of sentimental humanitarianism, which is not in accord with our harsh epoch. The necessary instructions will there-

fore be issued this very day to General Ambrosio, giving a completely free hand to the French police in this matter. [19]

As proof of his intentions, Mussolini subsequently sent Guido Lospinoso, a former police inspector from Bari, to establish a Commissariat for Jewish Affairs at Nice. Lospinoso was a personal acquaintance of the prime minister, with a reputation for efficiency and energy. The Italian message to the Germans was clear. If Italian Foreign Ministry and military officials were reluctant to cooperate with German demands, the Italian police and the notoriously more anti-Semitic Ministry of the Interior would simply bypass them. The Germans were delighted. Heinrich Müller, chief of the Gestapo, stated from Berlin on April 2 that Lospinoso would "regulate the Jewish problems . . . in accordance with the German conception, and in the closest collaboration with the German police." Lospinoso had, Müller added, already been in France for several days. [20]

Another brief comedy began. On April 5, SS Colonel Dr. Helmut Knochen, chief of German security police in Paris, informed Berlin that "nothing is known of [Lospinoso's] journey." [21] On April 7, Müller in Berlin insisted that "Lospinoso has been in France for some days." [22] By April 8, Knochen had finally learned that Lospinoso had been in Menton for three days, but had returned to Rome. [23] A month and a half later, on May 24, Knochen was still complaining that "we know nothing of [Lospinoso's] possible presence in the Italian zone." [24]

On May 26, relieved SS agents in France finally discovered that Lospinoso had set up headquarters in a villa near Nice. The man himself, however, remained elusive. As late as June 23, Knochen complained that Lospinoso was still "evading a visit to the Supreme Chief of the SS . . . yet at the same time establishing contact with the Chief of the French Police about the application of the anti-Jewish measures."[25] Then on July 7, Lospinoso failed to appear at an arranged meeting with German security police in Marseilles. He sent a representative, who immediately declared that he had no authority to make decisions about the Jewish question. The Germans would have to speak with Lospinoso himself![26]

As in Croatia, however, Italian authorities realized that some action was required to appease German wrath. Thus between May and the September 8 armistice, they intensified their efforts to send Jews away from coastal areas to enforced residence in the interior. The Nazis were far from satisfied. They complained that the transferred Jews were lodged in luxury hotels in fashionable spas, while the thousands remaining along the Côte d'Azur dined in the best restaurants, lived comfortably, and attempted to undermine Italian-German friendship. There was an element of truth in their charges, but Italian authorities could again claim that they were trying.

Mussolini's fall in July did not alter Lospinoso's official status, but it did provide him with a welcome excuse for further delay. He carefully informed the Germans on August 18 that he would have to return to Rome for new instructions. In fact, however, the nature of his problems had changed, for the Badoglio government, anticipating the still secret armistice, decided in August to withdraw from most of occupied France. The Italian army would attempt to hold only a vastly reduced area around Nice. On August 28, Italian officials agreed that the Jews should be allowed to accompany the army when it withdrew. Jewish relief agencies hired fifty trucks to bring refugees in Haute Savoy back to Nice and, they believed, to safety.

The Badoglio period also witnessed the Herculean efforts of Angelo Donati, a Jewish Italian from Modena, to organize a massive rescue operation. Donati had served as a liaison officer between the French and Italian armies during World

The Italians and The Holocaust

War I. After the war, he had helped found and direct a French-Italian bank in Paris. He became involved with German Jewish refugee relief after 1933. When the Germans occupied northern France in 1940, he moved to Nice and dedicated his considerable talents to refugee assistance.[27]

Donati's activities span the entire period of Italian occupation in southern France. In December 1942, when the prefect of Alpes-Maritimes wanted to evacuate foreign Jews into a German-occupied department, Donati first alerted Italian authorities. In March 1943, when Lospinoso arrived in Nice to begin his duties as commissar for Jewish affairs, Donati met, befriended, and advised him. Donati cooperated fully in the transfer of foreign Jews from Nice to enforced residence in Haute Savoy—a move that temporarily stalled the Germans and located Jews near the Swiss and Italian frontiers. Donati subsequently petitioned the Badoglio government to permit those same Jews to withdraw with the Italian army back into the soon-to-be reduced occupation zone around Nice.

Donati knew that thousands of Jews could not remain permanently concentrated around Nice, practically surrounded by Germans and totally dependent on the protection of the crumbling Italian army. During the last days of August and the first week of September, he made a last heroic effort to save his people. On the morning of September 8, after desperate negotiations with Italian officials, British and U.S. representatives at the Vatican, and the American Joint Distribution Committee, he established a rescue plan: the Badoglio government agreed to provide four ships, the British and Americans agreed to permit thirty thousand Jews from France to land in North Africa, and the "Joint" agreed to finance the vast move. The armistice, signed by Badoglio, was not scheduled to be made public until the end of the month. The ships would sail well before then.[28]

The premature announcement of the armistice caught everyone but the Germans unprepared, destroying all hope of implementing Donati's plan. The Italians clearly could not hold Nice, or even keep the Germans out of their own country. The army immediately disintegrated and Italian soldiers scrambled back across their frontier. As in Croatia and Greece during the same period, the Jews were left unprotected.

The Nazis entered Nice on September 9, angry and determined to take revenge for the ten months of Italian interference with their Final Solution. In addition to more than five thousand French Jews living in Nice at the time, there were at least sixteen thousand Jewish refugees in the city officially, and probably another two thousand there unofficially. At least another two thousand had left their enforced residences and descended on Nice in the early days of September, as rumors of the reduced Italian zone and Donati's escape plan filtered through the countryside. Most of the refugees were foreigners. They did not speak French. They knew no one in Nice. They had no plans, no hiding places, and with the disintegration of the Jewish relief agencies, no money. They were totally helpless.

The Jews of Nice, French and foreign alike, were caught in the most ruthless manhunt of the war in Western Europe. For more than a week, the Nazis searched every hotel and boarding house in the city, room by room. They also searched all trains leaving the city, so no one could escape. They ignored even valid documents, arresting and beating people who simply "looked Jewish." They physically searched every male, and sent every circumcised victim, together with all the men, women, and children in his household, to the notorious French holding camp at Drancy. From there, the trains left for Auschwitz. For 1,326 desperate refugees and 494 Jews born in France, a long odyssey of escape reached a terrible conclusion. The Italians had given them only a brief respite.[29]

Jews still in the French countryside on September 8 fared

somewhat better. While many were caught and deported when the Germans entered the Italian zone, some escaped into the mountains and joined the French partisans. Others hid with French families or crossed the border to Switzerland. About 1,100 others, too far from Switzerland, followed the retreating Italian army across another frontier, hoping to find an Italy at peace. They entered, instead, a country as strictly occupied as the one they had left. In the next year and a half, their fate became linked with that of the Jews of Italy.

Many of the Jews to follow the Italian army after the armistice left from Saint-Martin-Vésubie, a French village located 60 kilometers north of Nice and just a few kilometers from two mountain passes leading into northern Italy. Saint-Martin lay at an altitude of 1,000 meters above sea level. The nearby passes were both over 2,400 meters. At least 225 Jews lived in enforced residence in Saint-Martin, but over a thousand panic-stricken refugees collected there as the news of the Italian collapse spread. [30]

Between September 8, the date of the Italian armistice, and September 13, when the Germans arrived to stop the exodus, about 1,000 men, women, and children fled from Saint-Martin over the rugged passes into Italy. For the strongest, the flight lasted five or six hours; for the old and the very young—and there were many—it was much longer. One man, who later died of a heart attack in an Italian hospital, was eighty-four, and several babies, born in Saint-Martin, were under a year. Some refugees traveled in groups and some in small family units. Many accompanied the hundreds of Italian soldiers who had chosen the same flight. Soldiers helped carry their luggage and even their babies. [31]

The exhausted refugees and soldiers came out of the passes into two little Italian villages, Valdieri and Entraque, in the province of Cuneo southwest of Turin. They were treated kindly, fed bread and coffee, and given two large rooms where they could sleep on straw on the floor. One survivor remembers, "Our hearts filled again with hope: the Italians were so good, everything would work out for the best." [32] As their panic eased, they began to wonder why they had come. Alfred Feldman explains that they had vaguely expected the Germans to occupy France and the Americans, Italy. [33] But in Valdieri and Entraque, the Americans were not to be seen. Ominously, the Germans had occupied nearby Cuneo on September 12.

Most refugees finally realized that Valdieri and Entraque, however friendly, were dangerous traps. The Nazis, aware of the mountain passes, would soon come looking for them there. The youngest and strongest quickly left the two villages to hide in the mountains. Many others could run no longer. Winter was coming. Children and old people, with no money and no heavy clothing, could not survive in the wilderness. They found lodgings in the two villages.

On the morning of September 18, a poster appeared in villages near the passes, demanding that all foreigners present themselves to the German SS occupying forces by 6:00 P.M. that night, on pain of death. Italians protecting foreigners, the poster added, would also be shot. [34] The original text of the poster apparently used the word "Jew" instead of foreigner. The SS realized, however, that most local residents had never seen a Jew and would scarcely understand the term. Foreigners were more easily recognizable.

To encourage surrender, one SS soldier was sent to Valdieri and one to Entraque. Together they arrested about 349 Jewish refugees from southern France. These 349 included at least 119 Poles, 56 French, 42 Germans, 34 Hungarians, 25 Austrians, 22 Belgians, and 20 Rumanians. [35] Many had been eluding the Nazis for years. In country after country, they had found the courage to give up homes or temporary refuges to flee again. Now the Nazis reached them even in the remote mountain valleys of northern Italy. They had no more strength to run.

Natan Frankel, a thirty-three-year-old engineer from Warsaw, personally led a group over the Alps. On September 18, he learned that his entire group planned to give themselves up. The local family sheltering him and his wife urged him to remain in hiding. He insisted that his place was with his people. He and his wife surrendered. They both died at Auschwitz.[36]

The 349 were taken to an old army barracks in Borgo San Dalmazzo, the nearest town. There they were held under guard for two months. A few managed to escape, and many fell ill and were taken to nearby hospitals. On November 21, 1943, about 330 were deported. Their sealed boxcars carried them back to Nice, then to Drancy, and finally, in December and January, to Auschwitz. No more than 9 are known to have survived.[37]

On the gray November morning when the prisoners marched to the boxcars that were to carry them back to France and ultimately to Auschwitz, parish priest Don Raimondo Viale of Borgo San Dalmazzo stood on his church steps with a friend, watching helplessly. The priest had recently been imprisoned as an anti-Fascist. He was at that moment hiding about thirty Jews from France in his church, and he could not endanger them. His friend was freer to act. A mother with two young daughters, ages five and seven, marched past. The man recognized them, for their father, also a prisoner, had been in the local hospital. Profiting from a moment of inattention on the part of the SS guards, the man tried to lure the two children away from the group. The mother had spent years eluding the Nazis in France. Now she saw the attempt, failed to understand, and began to scream. She reclaimed her daughters, and they marched on to their deaths.[38]

About 750 refugees remained in the mountains of the province of Cuneo. Their story during the year and a half that followed is a replica of the experiences of Jews in occupied Italy generally. Many received help in one form or another from the exceptional Don Viale. The parish priest found hiding places, provided false documents, and distributed funds essential for survival. He and trusted assistants, many of them local parish priests, also accompanied many refugees to Genoa. There they introduced them to Don Francesco Repetto, secretary to the archbishop, Cardinal Pietro Boetto. Don Repetto lodged the refugees in seminaries, monasteries, and convents throughout the city, where they waited for guides to take them to Switzerland or south to the Allied lines. [39]

Most of the funds that Don Viale distributed came originally from the American Joint Distribution Committee. Deposited first in London, they were transferred to Rome with the help of the British ambassador to the Vatican. Those destined for the Jews from Saint-Martin-Vésubie were sent first to Don Repetto in Genoa, then to Don Viale in Borgo, and finally to parish priests in tiny villages throughout the province of Cuneo. [40]

Some money was also distributed by Delasem delegates under conditions that defy the imagination. Most early Delasem couriers were Jewish, and they had to travel on trains where control agents demanded to see their false documents. Body searches were not infrequent. Couriers needed explanations for their large amounts of money and for their presence in remote areas. They also needed nerves of steel. Not surprisingly, as networks of courier-priests developed, they tended to replace Jewish couriers. The priests pretended the funds were for the distribution of parish news bulletins in isolated areas.

Don F. Brondello, assistant parish priest of tiny Valdieri, tells the story of a distinguished-looking, elderly gentleman named Guido De Angeli who appeared at his church one autumn day with Delasem funds. De Angeli asked the priest if, when he distributed the money, he would remind the recipients that the next day was Yom Kippur. "I didn't know exactly what that word meant," Don Brondello relates, "But I obeyed the request precisely. In every case, at the word Kippur I saw many faces brighten, and I heard many affectionate words directed toward De Angeli."[41]

In addition to the priests and the Delasem delegates, many other Italians offered assistance to the Jews of Saint-Martin. Giuseppe Tiburzio, an Italian officer, convinced a Belgian Jewish father that his nine-year-old daughter, Paola Gotlieb, could not survive the winter in an open mountain hut at an altitude of 1,700 meters. After promising the father to raise the girl in the Jewish faith, he took her to his parents in Venice. The father was caught and died at Auschwitz. Paola survived, and the Tiburzio family, despite their love for her, gave her up to an aunt living in England after the war. In 1955, Giuseppe Tiburzio wrote, "What I did appeared then, as now, perfectly natural, and I believe that in my place, many others would have done the same."[42]

Other Italians tried to escort Jews into Switzerland. Luciano Elmo, a Milanese lawyer, recalls the supreme difficulty of trying to move foreigners through public places in a country teeming with Italian and German police. Elmo had taken refuge from the bombing of Milan in his wife's house in Borgo. When the Jews of Saint-Martin came down from the mountain passes, thirty found lodgings with him. He provided them with false documents and then, in groups of five or six, took them by train to Milan, en route to Switzerland. He remembers:

> We used to leave Borgo on the 4:15 morning train. I distributed one Jew in each car, with instructions to pretend to sleep; thus if a control agent came, they could produce their false identity

cards with a sleepy air. Not one of them spoke a single word of Italian. [43]

In some cases, even government bureaucrats from Mussolini's puppet regime at Salò seem to have treated Jewish refugees with consideration. Letters of thanks from the Jews of Saint-Martin who hid in the commune of Demonte during the last year of the war expressed gratitude to officials of the prefecture and even to the local marshal of the *carabinieri*. [44]

Not all Italians, of course, acted with courage or even common decency, and not all refugees survived. Several were caught and deported. Several others were executed in the province of Cuneo as real or supposed partisan activists. Sometimes the executioners were Germans; sometimes they were Italians. The last and perhaps most terrible atrocity to befall the Jews from Saint-Martin occurred at the very end of the war, and was a purely Italian affair. On the evening of April 25, 1945, Fascist militiamen seized six Jewish refugees from a prison at Cuneo, where they had been held since their arrests that spring, and murdered them in cold blood. The oldest was fifty-three; the youngest, only seventeen. They had crossed the Alps in September 1943. Italy had represented their last hope of survival, and Italy had, in the end, failed them. [45]

Leaving aside for the moment the many Italians at home who aided or failed to aid Jews, the behavior of Italian officials in occupied territories remains to be explained. Why did they act as they did? The Jews they helped were not friends, neighbors, or even co-nationals. Their own government was officially anti-Semitic. They themselves had shown no heroic tendency to protest when Italian Jews were forced out of the army or the Foreign Ministry. They had stood by when police shipped foreign Jews in Italy to internment camps. Why, when Germans tried to deport foreign Jews, did they behave differently?

The Italians and The Holocaust

It should be noted that most Italians dealing with Jews abroad probably had no direct experience with anti-Semitism at home. The tiny size of the Jewish community—one-tenth of 1 percent of the population—and its concentration in larger cities meant that most Italian soldiers and diplomats, like most Italians generally, knew almost no Jews at all. They may or may not have found the racial laws distasteful and the Ministry of the Interior bureaucrats who enforced them reprehensible. But one rarely risks a career to protest something one has not directly experienced.

On the other hand, Italians in the occupied territories faced an enormous "Jewish problem" every single day. They could not ignore the massacres of Jews and Serbs in Croatia, the roundups and deportations in Croatia and Greece, or the manhunts for thousands of destitute refugees in southern France. Furthermore, the implications of the problem were overwhelmingly different, for if in Italy Jews were being persecuted, in the occupied territories they were clearly being murdered. In 1941 and early 1942, Italian soldiers in Croatia acted spontaneously to save Jews and Serbs from murder on the spot. By mid-1942, when Nazis began to demand Croatian and Greek Jews for "resettlement in the East," most Italian diplomats and officers understood that deportation also meant murder.[46] The distinction between internment camps in southern Italy and "resettlement in the East" was a distinction between hardship and death. While Italians might overlook the first, they would not abet the second.

The peculiar blend of little direct experience of anti-Semitism at home and daily contact with persecution and murder abroad explains statements by Italian officials that would otherwise smack of hypocrisy or outright lying. For example, an Italian chief of staff in Mostar, near the Dalmatian coast, refused to permit deportation of Jews from that city on the grounds that Italians granted full equality to all residents.[47]

Italians and Jews in the Occupied Territories

After 1938, that clearly was not true. An Italian consul general in southern France, when denying a similar demand, stated that he would apply the same legislation as at home, for it was "a humane legislation."[48] It is hard to label internment camps, expulsion from professions and schools, and denial of nationality "humane," but that official may never have seen his country's racial laws at work. He had surely seen victims of anti-Semitism in southern France.

Nevertheless, Italian officials might have stood aside. After all, French bureaucrats, German army officers, and thousands of frightened, ambitious, or merely indifferent public officials in other occupied countries simply pretended they did not know about, or could not influence, events. Even most Italians, when the Germans in turn occupied their country, chose to ignore the deportations. Why did Italians abroad act differently?

The Jewish question in the occupied territories was intricately related to Italian perceptions of their own honor, prestige, and independence in the Axis partnership. That image had suffered greatly since the beginning of the war and the revelation of Italian military weakness. The German army had bailed out the Italians twice, in Greece in April 1941, and in North Africa later the same year. Italian pride had been hurt, and public officials were sensitive to challenges to Italian sovereignty.

Nor were the challenges imaginary. In all areas where Italians ultimately resisted German demands for the Jews, they already nursed grievances against their ally. In Croatia, Italians had expected to occupy the entire new state, only to be forced to divide it with the Germans. Adding insult to injury, the Germans and the Croats then made a deal to deport Croatian Jews without even consulting the Italians. In Greece, the Germans had easily taken Athens in April 1941, after the Italian military stalemate. They then delivered it to

The Italians and The Holocaust

the Italians for occupation. Humiliating Nazi interference in Athens continued, and German-sponsored groups of Greek students attacked Jews there throughout the period of Italian occupation. In southern France after November 1942, Italy had occupied most of the region east of the Rhône with little difficulty, but actual jurisdiction in the departments nearest the German zone was often unclear. Significantly, it was in this border area, in Ardèche and Drôme, that Italian, German, and French differences over the treatment of Jews in France first emerged.

Italian diplomats and military officers, with their injured pride and their grievances against the Germans, were determined to resist any demand that appeared as an encroachment upon their sovereignty. German demands for the Jews clearly fell into that category. Furthermore, Italians feared that submission to those demands would weaken their authority over the occupied peoples and complicate the job of maintaining order. In both Croatia and southern France, they were dealing with nominally autonomous governments that wanted to cooperate with German deportation decrees. Italian acquiescence would have reduced their own role to that of a mere accomplice. In addition, in Greece and southern France where a majority of the population remained mildly sympathetic to the Jews, Italian opposition to deportations could serve as a wedge between citizens and local pro-Nazi contenders for power. In all areas, Italian submission to German deportation demands would have made them look like weak junior partners in the Axis alliance, unworthy of the respect of those they meant to rule.

To some extent, their first spontaneous responses to the Jewish question also committed Italians to consistent resistance to German demands. Thus, in Croatia, after Italian soldiers rescued Jews from Ustasha terrorists, it would have been difficult for Italian officers to deliver them up for deportation later. Local Croatians would have concluded that the Italians were afraid of the Germans. Similarly, in southern France, after Italian officials publicly opposed the transfer of foreign Jews from the Italian to the German-occupied zone for internment—a decision probably made as much to insure Italian authority over Nazi and French police as to safeguard Jews— it was difficult to alter that policy. Concessions or changes would appear as weakness.

Finally, some evidence exists that with regard to Jews in the occupied territories, Italian officials acted with an eye on a future reckoning of accounts. By early 1943, many knew the horrors that resettlement in the East entailed. By about the same time, German defeats at Stalingrad and in Africa left little doubt about the outcome of the war to all but the most fanatic. Italy shared with Germany an ideology and a responsibility for an aggressive war. Many of her less fanatic leaders did not wish to share responsibility for the Holocaust as well.

But when all is said, something still seems missing. Bureaucrats in other nations suffered wounded pride, yet often hastened to ingratiate themselves with those in power. As late as 1944, Hungarian bureaucrats who knew the war was lost and were not yet implicated in Nazi atrocities did not hesitate to deliver their own, not foreign, Jews for deportation. Furthermore, from the Italian point of view there were often good reasons why protection of the Jews was not in the best interest of officials or of the country at large. Resistance to German demands not only jeopardized personal careers, but weakened the whole alliance on which Italian security during the war depended.

When all the logical reasons for and against cooperation in the Holocaust are weighed and measured, it is apparent that decency, courage, and humanity often tipped the balance. The soldiers who instinctively saved Jews and Serbs from the Ustasha did not act merely from calculation or a dislike of Germans.

The Italians and The Holocaust

Italians who issued passports to Greek Jews with Italian-sounding names in Salonika or went to internment camps to claim their "wives" were not motivated by threats to their nation's sovereignty, for Salonika was clearly in the German zone. Italian officials during the confused Badoglio period who remembered to instruct authorities on Arbe not to release interned Jews to the Croats unless Jews themselves requested it, and who negotiated frantically to find places for those same Jews in Italy, were no longer motivated by injured pride or concerns of sovereignty. They were preparing to abandon Croatia, and were acting to save lives. Italian peasant soldiers who carried Jewish children over the Alps from France to Italy would not have understood complicated behavioral analysis. They too were acting to save lives. Not the lives of friends, neighbors, coreligionists, or countrymen. Just lives.

Italian soldiers, officers, and diplomats in Croatia, Greece, and southern France restored a glimmer of honor to the shabby history of Fascist Italy. They proved that many Italians had not succumbed to twenty years of Fascist rhetoric. In the darkest hours of the Holocaust, they proved that some Christians in public positions cared about the fate of the Jews and were willing to act. They were brave, decent, and far too few.

6

Rome, 1943:
The October Roundup

ROMANS venturing into the streets near the old Jewish ghetto in the early hours of Saturday, October 16, 1943,
must have understood instantly that the relative tranquillity of
the first six weeks of German occupation had ended. In the
rainy darkness, German SS security police were surrounding an
area of several blocks lying adjacent to the ancient Roman
Theater of Marcellus and across the Tiber from Trastevere.
The area housed about four thousand of Rome's twelve thousand Jews. After blocking passages in and out of the ghetto, the
SS struck. It was 5:30 A.M., and most people were still asleep.

As armed guards outside every building fired indiscrimi-
nately to keep residents inside, two or three SS men pounded
on doors. On entering apartments, they immediately cut any
existing telephone wires. Then they ordered inhabitants into
the street. Foggy with sleep and often still in their night
clothes, the terrified victims had no choice but to obey.

The Italians and The Holocaust

Despite the darkness and the confusion, few escaped. Some young men, believing the raid to be a labor conscription, fled along the rooftops. Two courageous mothers, together in an apartment with four young children, barricaded the door with a heavy marble table and crouched behind it. In silent terror, they waited while the SS tried to break in. Finally convinced that no one was home, the police left and the women and children were safe. [1] There were few other fortunate exceptions that tragic morning. More common was the case of forty-four-year-old Settimio Calò. He had left his home before dawn to queue for cigarettes. When he returned, he discovered that his wife and nine children were gone. Their beds were still warm. [2]

Once in the streets, many were immediately herded into waiting trucks. Such was the case with the family of Marco Miele, a baby of about eighteen months. As the truck drove off, the cries of an old aunt who had been left behind aroused the pity of an unknown Catholic woman passing by. She screamed to the Nazis that the baby was hers, and a Catholic. They believed her, and Marco Miele was saved. [3]

Many other victims in the old ghetto were herded toward the ruins of the Theater of Marcellus, where they waited in their night clothes in the rain and the cold. The old and the sick could barely stand. Children wailed. Families, trying to stay together, clung to each other desperately. SS guards pushed and shoved. An employee at a nearby government ministry on his way to work that morning described it as a scene out of purgatory. "Everywhere the pleas and heartrending cries of the victims could be heard, while their captors, whether violent or impassive, performed their sorry task without showing any sign of human pity." [4] Eventually trucks carried off the last of the waiting groups, and the deserted streets were silent.

Other SS police armed with lists of the names and addresses

of Jews living outside the ghetto methodically visited individual apartments. They also began early, about 5:30 A.M. They usually handed their victims written instructions, printed in German and Italian. The orders explained that the Jews had twenty minutes in which to pack food for eight days, two blankets, money, jewelry, and valuables. They were going on a long trip. Meanwhile, a police car or truck waited outside.

Twenty-nine-year-old Arminio Wachsberger, his wife Regina, and their five-year-old daughter lived just across the Tiber from the old ghetto. His neighborhood, Trastevere, housed another three thousand Roman Jews. When the SS knocked on Wachsberger's door, his two-year-old nephew was also with him. All were forced into a truck. As the truck stopped in front of his brother-in-law's building, Wachsberger took advantage of a brief moment of SS inattention to hand the boy over to the janitor's wife. "Thus," he remembered later (he was one of the handful of survivors), "the child was saved, while my daughter would die with her mother in the gas chambers at Auschwitz." [5]

As the SS police ventured away from the predominantly Jewish neighborhoods of the old ghetto and Trastevere, arrests became more difficult. Emanuele Sbaffi, a Methodist minister, was working in his office on the fourth floor of his apartment building when he saw two SS police with fixed bayonets guarding the outside door. Descending to his apartment on the second floor, he intercepted two Jewish women whose elderly father had just been arrested in front of the building. He pushed the women into his living room. The SS knocked on his door to ask about the Jewish tenants on their list. He replied evenly that he thought they had all gone away. His two fugitives were saved. Meanwhile, two other Jewish women in the next apartment jumped from their back window and also escaped. [6]

Piero Modigliani and his family were equally fortunate. At

The Italians and The Holocaust

8:30 A.M., Piero received a telephone call from a close, non-Jewish friend giving him a prearranged word of warning. After alerting his mother and brother in another apartment in the same building, he and his wife left immediately. His mother and brother, not quick enough, were still at home when the German SS police arrived. They simply did not open the door, and their doorman convinced the Nazis that they had left town. Afraid that the police, still waiting in the street, might return to break into the apartment, they descended to the ground floor and entered a typing school by an interior doorway. There, with the full knowledge of the students, they joined the class![7]

Many were not so lucky. Admiral Augusto Capon, the seventy-one-year-old father-in-law of Enrico Fermi, was captured that morning. Half paralyzed from an illness incurred in military service, he had to be carried to the car.[8] Alina Cavalieri, a distinguished sixty-one-year-old woman who had won a silver medal in World War I for nursing services at the front, was also taken.[9] The wife of Commendator Giuseppe Segre, about eighty, was seized from her sick bed.[10] Lionello Alatri, owner of one of Rome's largest department stores and prominent member of the Jewish Council, was arrested with his wife and her ninety-year-old father.[11] Arminio Wachsberger remembers many doctors and professors among the prisoners. The October 16 roundup had reached well beyond the ghetto into all social and economic groups. Altogether, 365 German SS police had arrested 1,259 people before the action ended nine hours later.[12]

Why were so many people caught asleep in their own apartments in the sixth week of the German occupation of Rome? They knew the 1938 government census of Italian Jews, constantly updated by Fascists during the war, had fallen into German hands. Were they unaware of the fate of Jews in other occupied countries? Wachsberger explains, "From Radio London we had learned about the existence of concentration camps and the provisions against the Jews but, to tell the truth, we did not believe much: we thought all these stories were matters of Allied propaganda against the Germans." [13] Stories of German atrocities during World War I had turned out to be untrue, and so, it was hoped, would these.

But had no one heard of the massacres of Jews around Lago Maggiore, or the arrests of Jewish refugees escaping into Italy from France? Surely some had. Perhaps they dismissed the stories as actions against foreign, not Italian, Jews. Since September 23, after all, most of Italy had been reorganized as the Italian Social Republic (RSI), under the nominal leadership of Mussolini himself. Freed from an Italian prison by German SS commandos on September 12, Mussolini had become a Nazi tool and ally. But he had not released Jews for deportation in the past, and they now hoped he would continue to protect them. They overlooked the limited nature of Italian autonomy.

The fears of Roman Jews were also lulled by the presence of the Pope in Vatican City. They knew, of course, that Pope Pius XII was hardly their staunch defender. [14] He had not opposed the Italian racial laws. He had not condemned occasional Catholic press articles and bishops' speeches approving religious, if not racial, discrimination. He had not tried to protect Jews in other European countries. But in Rome itself, Vatican officials had often been quietly sympathetic.

Every Roman Jew could cite cases of Vatican good will. Some individuals who had lost jobs because of the racial laws found employment there. Others who wished to emigrate received assistance. Jewish high school graduates interested in law but rejected by Italian universities for racial reasons were accepted at the Pontificium Institutum Utriusque Iuris. Fabio Della Seta remembers it as "the only Roman university institution where, in those days [1938–43], a language of almost absolute liberty could be spoken." [15] The language was Latin. Surely the Pope, a world-wide symbol of benevolence who offered employment, aid, and education to all Romans, would not allow Jews to be arrested and deported under his very windows.

Even more reassuring were the attitudes and behavior of the leaders of the Roman Jews. Dante Almansi, national president of the Union of Italian Jewish Communities, and Ugo Foà, president of the Jewish Community of Rome, have appeared earlier in this book. The former had been a vice-chief of police under Mussolini; the latter, a high-ranking magistrate. Both were conscientious civil servants whose private lives were above reproach. Both were well-connected Fascist party members who nevertheless lost their jobs because of the racial laws. Both decided then to dedicate themselves to the Italian Jewish community. Almansi served the union brilliantly, restoring order to an organization torn by dissent on the question of reconciling fascism with Zionism. With his many connections in high places, he was also instrumental in obtaining government permission to establish Delasem for the aid of foreign Jewish refugees. Foà, too, won concessions for his people, and with his integrity and dedication, he won their respect. [16]

After the German occupation, Almansi and Foà decided that Rome's Jewish Community should continue to function exactly as before. They refused to close the synagogue, or to stop or even reduce the number of services. They discouraged the circulation of alarming information. They had certainly heard rumors of the Holocaust. Settimio Sorani, local Delasem representative, later testified that "I knew then [mid-1943] as much as is known today. Everything." [17] He had listened to the refugees he was assisting, and he pleaded with Almansi and Foà to warn the Jews of Rome. They refused.

The motivation of Almansi and Foà remains a matter of speculation. Critics say they were reluctant to disperse the community upon which their power and status depended, without clear cause. The more charitable suggest that their decision was a natural product of their personalities and careers. They were conservative, cautious, rational men conditioned to believe that deals were always possible, that everything could be manipulated, and that the ruling class, at least in the short run, usually kept its word. Their apologists explain that they were determined to avoid provoking the Nazis, as the closing of the synagogue and the disappearance of the Jews might have done. They also stress the difficulty of finding hiding places so early in the occupation, before Christian rescuers understood the full depth of the danger and before false documents were available. [18]

Perhaps there is some truth in all three explanations. Like so many others, Almansi and Foà retained their faith in Mussolini and the Pope, and they feared the consequences of panic and disorder. They knew that hiding places were not easy to secure, especially for the poor, and that people caught hiding where they did not live could be arrested. Also, they knew that abandoned property could be confiscated. Hiding seemed premature. And in any case, they thought, the Allies would soon reach Rome.

To their faith in Mussolini, the Pope, and their leaders, Roman Jews added another dimension common to European Jews everywhere. The memoirs of survivors constantly echo the same phrases: "We thought it could never happen here. We had done nothing wrong. We were always loyal citizens." Polish Jews thought it could only happen in Germany. German Jews thought it could only happen in Poland. Dutch and Belgian Jews thought it could only happen in the East. French Jews thought it could only happen to foreigners in France. Italian Jews, who looked, spoke, and worked exactly like their Christian neighbors and who had known so little anti-Semitism in the past, thought it could happen anywhere but in civilized

Italy. They had always been loyal Italians, and the concept of undeserved punishment was inconceivable. To some extent, they were simply believing what they desperately wanted to believe. On the other hand, the reality of the Final Solution defied the imaginations of all pre-Holocaust Europeans, often until the gas began to flow.

Throughout September and October 1943, Roman Jews made the private, agonizing decisions upon which their lives would soon depend. Silvana Ascarelli Castelnuovo, with her five children and her parents, went from convent to convent until she found places for everyone. She and her family would survive the October roundup and the war. [19] Author and publisher Luciano Morpurgo quietly stored food and blankets in a room in a distant neighborhood, and remained at home as long as possible. [20] He, too, would survive. Piero Modigliani rented a room in a modest pension, but delayed moving until he narrowly escaped the October 16 roundup. Several of his friends, most of them affluent Jews who could afford it, acted similarly. On September 29, Modigliani noted in his diary a joke that was circulating in Rome. Tourists ask their guide where Michelangelo's statue of Moses is. The guide replies, "For some days now, he has been in the home of friends." [21]

Despite the impression conveyed by the joke, many Roman Jews, perhaps the majority, did not hide at first. Like Arminio Wachsberger, most probably considered hiding, but ruled it out as inconvenient, expensive, and premature. The Germans were behaving in exemplary fashion. Surely warning signals would precede a roundup. Wachsberger's daughter was frail and sickly. He and his wife did not want to submit her to the rigors and deprivations of hiding. He would remain alert but at home. [22] His family did not survive.

For people like Wachsberger, not privy to inside information, respectful of their elders, anxious to survive, and in no way fatalistic, a warning from the Jewish leaders might have made all the difference. So, too, might a Papal condemnation of Nazi atrocities. The unbelievable might then have become real, and the step their instincts urged might have appeared essential. Some would not have fled under any circumstances—well after the October roundup, a few shattered, bewildered souls were caught still living in the old ghetto. But for the majority, official confirmation of their fears could have saved their lives.

While Roman Jews resolved to be watchful, the signs remained difficult to read. German soldiers treated civilians with courtesy and respect. They bought watches, cameras, and souvenirs from ghetto shopkeepers, paying the full price without quibbling. Jews were reassured, as the SS intended them to be. For the fate of the Jews had been decided. On September 12, SS Major (soon to become Lieutenant Colonel) Herbert Kappler, chief of the German security police in Rome, had received a telephone call from the Berlin office of SS Chief Heinrich Himmler, informing him that the Jews were to be deported. On September 25, Kappler received another message that said in part:

> All Jews, regardless of nationality, age, sex, and personal conditions must be transferred to Germany and liquidated. . . . The success of this undertaking will have to be ensured by a surprise action and for that reason it is strictly necessary to suspend the application of any anti-Jewish measures of an individual nature, likely to stir up among the population suspicion of an imminent action. [23]

Deception was the order of the day.

The first blow fell the following evening, when Almansi and Foà were summoned to a meeting in Kappler's office at 6:00 P.M. Kappler did not mince words. He informed the two men that the Germans considered Jews among their worst enemies, and would treat them as such. But, Kappler added, according to Foà:

> It is not your lives nor those of your children we will take, if you fulfill our demand. It is your gold we want to provide new arms for our nation. Within thirty-six hours you must bring me fifty kilograms of gold. If you do so, nothing bad will happen to you. If you do not, two hundred of you will be taken and deported to Germany. . . .[24]

Fifty kilograms of gold is the equivalent of more than 110 pounds. Kappler extended his deadline to forty and eventually to forty-four hours. During that period, Foà collected donations at his office at the synagogue. At first, word spread slowly, but by the afternoon of the first day, a long line had formed. Most of the richest Jews were in hiding or otherwise out of touch. Donations came mainly from Jews in the ghetto and Trastevere. Individuals gave a ring or two, or perhaps a single chain. Foà later recalled that the people "deprived themselves of every dear remembrance, every precious jewel to avoid the gigantic massacre."[25] Most receipts were for an eighth of an ounce. The line moved slowly; the gold accumulated still more slowly.

As word of the extortion spread, non-Jews, including some priests, joined the line. A Roman Jew present at the time later remembered:

> Circumspectly, as if fearing a refusal, as if afraid of offering gold to the rich Jews, some "Aryans" presented themselves. They entered that place adjacent to the synagogue full of embarrassment, not knowing if they should take off their hat or keep their head covered, according to the well-known Jewish custom. Almost humbly, they asked if they too could—well, if it would be right to. . . . Unfortunately, they did not leave their names.[26]

By 4:00 P.M. on Tuesday, September 28, fifty kilograms of gold had been delivered to Gestapo headquarters in Via Tasso, carefully weighed, and accepted. The Jews breathed a sigh of relief. The Germans had, after all, said they only wanted the gold, and the Germans were, most agreed, men of honor. The Jews were reassured, and the noose tightened another notch.

The idea to extort Jewish gold seems to have originated with Kappler, but his motives are subject to interpretation. In a deposition filed at the time of the trial of Adolf Eichmann, Kappler claimed that he had disapproved of the order to deport the Roman Jews. He never claimed opposition on moral grounds. Rather, he regarded the Jews as politically insignificant, and he was reluctant to risk popular and Vatican opposition unnecessarily. A police officer by profession, he preferred to use his victims as a source of money to finance espionage activities. He also believed them to be in contact with the Allies, and thus a source of valuable information. His gold extortion scheme, Kappler claimed, was intended to convince Himmler of the great potential in Jewish exploitation. [27]

A second interpretation of Kappler's motives is distinctly less charitable. Kappler knew that the unequivocal top-secret order for liquidation of the Jews had been intercepted by German army and diplomatic personnel in Rome. He had no idea how much farther the word had spread, but he knew that the Jews, once warned, would seek sanctuary in the hundreds of churches, monasteries, and convents throughout the city. His assigned task of capturing them would become much more difficult. He conceived of the gold extortion scheme with the specific intention of reassuring the Jews, until his preparations for a roundup were complete. [28]

The less charitable theory seems the more probable. Kappler may well have regarded deportation as a tactical error, but it is unlikely that he would have questioned his orders. It is equally unlikely that by September 1943, Kappler did not know that Himmler's SS fanatics were totally uninterested in mere exploitation of the Jews. The SS in Western Russia had demanded the systematic destruction of Jewish workers, farmers, artisans, and middle-class professionals—the only elements in an otherwise unskilled population who could effectively supply and sustain the German war effort there. Did Kappler really think they would act otherwise in Italy? Did he think Himmler would be impressed by fifty kilograms of gold when he had not recognized the labor potential of millions? After the war, the fifty kilograms of Roman gold were found in the office of Ernst Kaltenbrunner, chief of the Reich Security Main Office (RSHA). The box had never even been opened. [29]

The response of Pope Pius XII to the gold extortion is also subject to various interpretations. Apologists maintain that he was so outraged by the news that he immediately offered a gift of gold. Others go so far as to say that the gift was accepted. The facts as related by Foà, who was nothing if not respectful, deferential, even obsequious to all authority, are somewhat different.

> The Holy See, learning immediately of the fact [of the extortion], spontaneously made it known to the President of the Community [Foà himself] through official channels that if it was not possible to collect all the fifty kilograms of gold within the specified thirty-six hours he would place at his disposition the balance, which could be paid back later without hurry when the Community was in a condition to do so. [30]

This "noble gesture of the Vatican," Foà went on to say, was not needed, for he was able to collect the fifty kilograms of gold from other sources.

The Vatican offer, then, constituted a loan, not a gift, and even that contribution was contingent on the failure to collect gold from other sources. Furthermore, many individuals even question Foà's assertion that the offer was spontaneous. Renzo Levi, businessman and president of the Roman section of Delasem, related that he and another Jewish leader actually requested a Vatican loan during the first hours of the collection, when contributions were coming in slowly. The Pope authorized the loan, which was never needed. [31] Whether spontaneously offered or requested, the Vatican gesture was commendable, for it relieved Jewish leaders of their terrible fear of failure. As word of the offer spread, it also reassured Roman Jews and made them feel less alone. Unfortunately, it also confirmed their hope that, in the final analysis, the Pope would stand up for them.

If the extortion of gold temporarily eased Jewish fears of something worse, events the very next day revealed the emptiness of Kappler's promises. Early Friday morning, September 29, Kappler's security police surrounded the main synagogue, which also housed the Jewish Community's administrative offices. The Nazis claimed to be searching for compromising documents and correspondence with enemy agents. They found nothing of the sort, but they seized two million lire from the safe as well as vast archival materials. The Community's documents, registers, minutes of meetings, and records of contributors found their way to Gestapo headquarters. Entire file cabinets were transported intact. "A great truck," Foà recalled, "was scarcely sufficient for loading all the material." [32]

After the war, Foà insisted that the SS police had not obtained the detailed Community lists of members' names and addresses because he had hidden them elsewhere. Several witnesses have challenged this allegation; one man claimed to have found the lists at Gestapo headquarters after the liberation of Rome. [33] But even Foà admitted that the Nazis had seized records of contributors, and these in all likelihood included addresses as well as names. The details of September 29 are less important than the fact that all lists of names should have been destroyed. And the fact that the Nazis were interested in documents at all should have constituted a warning— the very sign of pending trouble that Roman Jews were looking for. Yet still no warning issued from the shambles of the Community offices. Instead, services went on as usual in the synagogue by the Tiber. It was the eve of Rosh Hashana.

During the days that followed, the pretense of normalcy continued. The actions of some might even be labeled active deception. Many of Rome's best-informed Jews went into hiding, but their decisions were never communicated to the masses around the old ghetto. The controversial chief rabbi of Rome, Israel Zolli, disappeared from view as early as September 18, after trying in vain to convince Foà to close the synagogue and warn the people. Born in Eastern Europe in 1881, the year of great Russian pogroms, Zolli had personal memories of anti-Semitism. As a rabbi in Trieste for nearly thirty years before coming to Rome in 1940, he had talked with hundreds of Jewish refugees from northern Europe during the 1930s. He was much more wary of the Nazis than most of his native Italian colleagues. His absence from Sabbath services on September 18 and from the observance of Rosh Hashana was vaguely attributed to illness. It was not allowed to constitute a warning.[34]

Almansi himself quietly changed apartments during the first week of October. No one was told. On October 10, the day following Yom Kippur, he also closed the office of the national Union of Italian Jewish Communities and removed the archives. Not wishing to cause alarm, he carefully explained that the war had disrupted communications between Jewish communities and made his office temporarily unable to function.[35] Excuses were similarly found for the individual, unexplained arrests of several Jews on October 9. These were "special cases," everyone agreed. The victims were anti-Fascists. The implication was clear. The innocent had nothing to fear.

Renzo Levi and Settimio Sorani, directors of Delasem in Rome, also went into hiding in early October. Again no one knew, although Sorani tried in vain to convince Foà of the danger. Delasem offices closed by October 10. As the main Delasem responsibility had always been the care of foreign Jewish refugees, however, Sorani took advantage of the lull before the storm to organize hiding places and clandestine assistance networks. He began in September 1943, with just over 100 refugees, all totally helpless without money, friends, or knowledge of Italian. By the time of the liberation of Rome nine months later, his "clients" numbered 1,500 foreigners, as well as 2,500 Italian Jews, often not Romans, who had abandoned their homes and needed help and support.[36]

Sorani's fugitives hid in churches, convents, and apartments throughout the city. They received identification cards, ration books, food, and money on a regular basis from secret visitors, usually priests mobilized after Sorani was forced to go underground and directed by a remarkable French Capuchin monk named Father Maria Benedetto.[37] Thanks to the efforts of Sorani, Father Benedetto, and the dedicated Italians who helped them, only about 100 of the approximately 1,800 Jews known to have been deported from Rome during the occupation were refugees.[38] Overall, foreign Jews fared better than the Roman Jews who had lived beside the Tiber for centuries.

On Wednesday, October 13, another blow struck the Jewish community. Two railroad cars rolled up on the trolley tracks and stopped in front of the synagogue. An Italian shipping company employee informed Foà that the Germans intended to seize the contents of his two libraries. Foà was not surprised. Several German scholars and soldiers had visited the libraries during the preceding days, confiscating catalogues and indexes and warning Foà that he must remove nothing, on pain of death. Now German soldiers carefully removed everything.

The loss of what Foà rightly called "Italian cultural patrimony" was staggering. The Library of the Roman Jewish Community contained, in his words, "manuscripts, incunabula,

The Italians and The Holocaust

. . . Eastern prints from the sixteenth century, unique copies of Jewish books, numerous important documents concerning the life of the Roman Community under papal domination from the first dawn of Christianity until 1870, etc. . . ."[39] Much material had been brought to Rome by Jews expelled from Spain and Sicily in the fifteenth century. The contents of the Rabbinical Library were less precious, but still significant. Now all this material of incalculable value was heading north in two fully loaded freight cars marked "Munich."

Three days after the plundering of the library, Rome's Jewish community was violated again. As previously described, the attackers this time consisted of 365 SS police and Waffen SS men, and they did not want gold or documents or books, but human beings.[40] By the time the October 16 action ended at 2:00 in the afternoon, 1,259 people, including 896 women and children, had been transported to a temporary detention center in the Italian Military College, only six hundred feet from Vatican City. There they remained under armed guard, while a crowd of curious onlookers gathered outside.

Because Arminio Wachsberger spoke German, the SS guards at the Military College immediately enlisted his services as an interpreter. His first assignment was to calm the terrified prisoners arriving in the college courtyard. Guards were pushing and shouting words that no one could understand. Wachsberger had to explain that the prisoners were all to be sent to a labor camp in the north. Those who were young and strong would have to work hard. The sick and the weak, the elderly and the children, would be assigned light jobs to earn their keep. The prisoners were soothed and became more manageable. By his own testimony after the war, Wachsberger himself believed the story.[41]

Among the prisoners at the Military College were numerous non-Jews, rounded up by mistake. Wachsberger helped the

Germans separate them from the others. All non-Jews, Wachsberger explained, were to present themselves to the SS guards. The penalty for lying would be immediate death. [42] Eventually, the special claims of 252 people were accepted. According to Kappler's report to Berlin, these consisted of the children of mixed marriages, spouses in mixed marriages including the Jewish partners, foreigners from neutral countries including one citizen of the Vatican, and "Aryan" servants and boarders who had been caught in Jewish homes. Because SS deportation measures at the time did not apply to individuals in these categories, they were released at dawn the following day. [43]

At least seven Jews also managed to slip into the non-Jewish group. Giuseppe Durghello, his wife Bettina, and their son Angelo, enjoyed the luxury of a "non-Jewish" last name. So did Enrico Mariani and, to a lesser extent, Angelo Dina. Wachsberger knew the truth, but he did not share it. Apparently the Nazis did not check claimants against their Community lists. The lucky ones were released. So, too, were Bianca Ravenna Levi and her daughter Piera. The sources do not explain their good fortune. Bianca had not one but two typically Jewish names! [44] Among those who remained, however, there was at least one non-Jew. A nurse charged with the care of a young epileptic Jewish boy chose not to abandon her charge. She died with him in the gas chambers at Auschwitz. [45]

Wachsberger remained busy throughout that Saturday afternoon and evening. He helped the guards record the names of the remaining 1,007 prisoners. Then he was ordered to inform them that because they were going to a labor camp where many would not be able to work, they must surrender their money and valuables to help support the weaker members. The penalty for refusal would be death. A long line formed. At first the prisoners gave up everything, for the welfare of all. Gradually, however, they observed that the most valuable items were disappearing into the guards' pockets. Word spread quickly down the line, and some prisoners managed to withhold a few treasures. [46]

By now it was nearly evening, and the lack of food became a problem. Many prisoners had brought nothing with them, and the Nazis had nothing to give. Some non-Jews and many courageous relatives of the prisoners had brought packages of food and clothing to the Military College, but the guards would allow no contributions. Instead, Wachsberger was instructed to collect the prisoners' apartment keys and go to their homes under armed guard to gather food. He thought that quite reasonable until he arrived at the apartments. Then he realized that his guards had no interest in food, but focused instead on thoroughly looting every home. [47]

At the college, hunger remained a problem, for many prisoners had not eaten all day. Wachsberger was given some of the money collected from the prisoners and sent again under guard to a nearby bakery. He was also allowed to buy medicines. [48] That must have reassured him and his people. Would the SS guards bother with medicine if they intended to murder their prisoners?

As night fell, the prisoners settled down and tried to rest. They had been assigned to various rooms, with the men apart from the women and children. A thin layer of straw covered the bare floor. Sanitary facilities scarcely existed. At least one young woman went into labor during the night, with her two children at her side. The Nazis summoned an Italian doctor, but they did not allow the mother to be transferred to a hospital. The baby was born in the courtyard. [49]

The thoughts of the prisoners that night can scarcely be imagined. To the sturdy poor, the prospect of a labor camp and regular employment was not totally negative. On the other hand, the old and the weak had few illusions about the rigors of life in a German camp, or about their ability to survive there.

Nevertheless, the promise of work offered at least a possibility of survival, and a thousand desperate minds focused eagerly on that slender hope.

The consequences of that hope cannot be exaggerated. In the days that lay ahead, several young people who might have escaped declined. One young man discovered an unbarred door in the Military College, left to buy cigarettes, and then returned to his wife and child. A group of young boys found themselves unguarded at a rest stop during the trip to Auschwitz. Several others rode north in a freight car with an unbarred window. Many more succeeded in breaking the lock on a freight car door, and rode for miles with the door open. Yet among all of these, only one young man chose to escape.[50]

Why did so many others not flee? Usually their decisions centered around their families. They did not want to be separated. They thought their families would need them in the labor camp. They did not wish to subject their families to collective reprisals for their own flight. Only the certainty of death for everyone at the end of the line could have convinced the young and the strong to attempt a break-out. But, as the Nazis intended, the Jews of Rome rejected that certainty despite everything they had heard about the fate of Jews in other countries.

Nor, on reflection, were their last illusions surprising. Why would the Nazis transport Jews hundreds of miles merely to kill them? Why would the Nazis kill them when they needed workers? Why would civilized people want to kill them in the first place? These questions have no rational answers, and the Jews were rational men and women. They could not conceive of the inconceivable.

Sunday, October 17, passed much like the afternoon and evening of the previous day. The non-Jewish prisoners were released at dawn. For the others, food and space remained in short supply. The questions, the rumors, and the fear continued.

At least one question was answered the following morning. Before dawn on October 18, trucks began to collect the Jewish prisoners at the Military College. As the trucks filled, they left to drive quickly across the city. Their destination was the cargo-loading platform at Rome's Tiburtina Station. The Jews did not pass through the normal passenger terminal.

At the station, a train with about twenty empty freight cars was waiting. As the trucks arrived, guards loaded their prisoners into the cars. As each car was filled to its capacity of fifty or sixty people, its door was slammed shut and locked from outside. The prisoners waited in darkness and terror while the trucks returned to the college for more victims. The earliest arrivals waited eight hours. Finally at about 2:00 P.M., the dreadful journey north began.[51]

Most prisoners on the train continued to believe they were going to a work camp. Arminio Wachsberger found himself in a car with Admiral Capon, who had a different opinion. "We are certainly going to our deaths," he declared, but no one believed him. "You don't know the Germans," he insisted. "I saw them in the First World War."[52]

Inside the crowded freight cars, conditions barely sustained human life. For light and air, most cars had only a single narrow window, barred and high up on the wall. The prisoners were so crowded they could scarcely all sit at the same time. Sanitary facilities did not exist. Desperate prisoners usually agreed to use one small area of the car as a toilet, and then struggled among themselves to find a place as far from that spot as possible. In many cars, people tried to shield the toilet area with some sort of covering for privacy, but most efforts were futile. Grown men and women wept from shame.

There was little food and no water. The first day of the

journey was very hot, and the prisoners' thirst soon became unbearable. The train stopped briefly at Orte, one hour out of Rome, where prisoners were allowed to descend to relieve themselves along the tracks. Only fifty did so; the others did not yet realize that no better arrangements would occur. After another hour, the train stopped briefly again, to remove the first dead prisoner. No one was allowed to descend.

The train reached Florence at 8:00 P.M., but the cars remained sealed. The hot day turned into a cold night as the train crossed the Appennines. Prisoners still in pajamas or light clothes shivered miserably. Finally at noon on Tuesday, October 19, the train crawled to an unscheduled stop at Padua. One car had mechanical problems and needed to be replaced. The other cars remained sealed. Prisoners, with nothing to drink for two days, began pleading for water.

A group of Fascist railroad militiamen who heard the cries asked why the prisoners could not be allowed to drink from several nearby fountains. "They are Jews," Wachsberger heard the SS guards replying, as if that explained everything. "Yes, but they are also people," insisted the Fascist militiamen.[53] An argument ensued. Finally, one of the Fascists raised his submachine gun and settled the issue. If the Jews were not allowed to get out and drink, he would shoot.[54] The Nazis submitted.

During the next two and a half hours, the freight cars were unsealed and several people from each car were selected to bring water to the others. Women from the Italian Red Cross were permitted to visit the cars and distribute food and medicine. At least two more dead bodies were removed. No one tried to escape. On the contrary, as the cars were closed and locked, several men and boys undetected in the confusion rushed to get back on the train. They did not want to be separated from their families.[55]

The death train left Padua on Tuesday afternoon and reached the Brenner Pass in the early hours of Wednesday,

The Italians and The Holocaust

October 20. In the frigid darkness, a German crew replaced the Italian one, the cars were opened, and the prisoners were carefully counted. The train then proceeded into Austria and Germany. Late Wednesday, it stopped outside Nuremberg. Women of the German Red Cross distributed hot barley soup to exhausted prisoners who had not eaten since noon of the previous day. One wonders what those women thought.

The train continued to roll eastward all day Thursday and Friday. At sunset on Friday, as the Sabbath began, the prisoners crossed their last frontier and entered Poland. Several more had died, including a young pregnant woman, but their bodies remained in the cars. Finally, about 11:00 P.M. Friday night, the train lurched to its last stop. It had reached Auschwitz too late for the prisoners to be admitted that night. They had been in captivity for almost a week. They had been on the train for five days and nights. Now they would wait until the morning of the Sabbath for the final chapter.

As the first morning light appeared over the camp, Arminio Wachsberger peered through the small barred window and saw huge barrage balloons over the camp. He lifted his five-year-old daughter up to see the balloons. An SS guard outside the train saw her little face at the window and threw a large rock straight at her. "After such an act of barbarity against that tiny, harmless human being," her father recalled, "I finally understood that we had arrived on the threshold of Hell."[56]

An hour or two later, the freight cars were unsealed, and the Jews of Rome were ordered to descend. Stiff, weak, and famished, many could hardly move. The infamous Dr. Josef Mengele himself was waiting for them on the platform. He addressed them through Wachsberger.

Mengele explained that the strongest were to walk to a work camp, where they would perform heavy labor. The sick and the weak, the elderly, and all young children and their mothers would be driven to a light labor camp to rest. All families,

Mengele explained, would be reunited each evening. The prisoners lined up, and Mengele himself made the selection.[57] He chose about 450 for heavy labor, and directed the others to the waiting trucks.

Then Mengele introduced a new factor. He explained to the 450 people chosen for labor that the walk to the work camp was about ten kilometers. Those who wanted to ride could join the others on the trucks. About 250 did so. At the conclusion of this second selection process, 149 men and 47 women remained.[58] They were duly admitted to the camp, disinfected, tattooed, and assigned prison garb. They never saw their loved ones again.

An entry in the Auschwitz log for October 23, 1943, one week after the roundup in Rome, states the situation precisely:

> RSHA—Transport, Jews from Rome. After the selection 149 men registered with numbers 158451–158639 and 47 women registered with numbers 66172–66218 have been admitted to the detention camp. The rest have been gassed.[59]

The rest, more than eight hundred people, were driven from the railroad platform directly to the Auschwitz killing center. Still mercifully unaware of their fates, they were divided into two large groups and forced to undress and enter a large sealed room where they would shower. There they died slowly in pools of blood, vomit, and defecation, as poison gas destroyed their respiratory systems.

By evening, over eight hundred people had disappeared in the roaring crematoria of Auschwitz. Only their hair and the gold from their teeth remained behind to serve the German war effort. Among the eight hundred were the wife of Arminio Wachsberger and the daughter who had not been allowed to enjoy the balloons. Among them also were the baby born at the Military College, its mother, and her other two children. Among them were the wife and nine children of Settimio Calò, the boys who had rejoined the train to save their families from reprisals, the father-in-law of Enrico Fermi, and many, many others. They never had time to wonder why they had to die, but even with time, they would have found no reason. There was no reason. They were Jews.

Several days later, Wachsberger asked Mengele about his wife and child. Incredibly enough, no one in the huge labor camp had told him about the gas chambers, and he had continued to hope that they were well. Mengele told him his family no longer existed. Weeping, Wachsberger asked him why. Mengele gave him the standard answer. "You are Jews."[60]

On a different occasion, Wachsberger asked Mengele another question. At the time of the selection on the railroad platform, Mengele had refused to allow Wachsberger to join his family on the trucks, explaining that he was needed as an interpreter. He set out on the ten-kilometer walk to the labor camp, only to discover that it was but half a kilometer. He asked Mengele why he had allowed so many strong young people to ride to their deaths when they had already passed the initial selection. They would have been capable of solid work. "They were lazy if they were afraid of a ten-kilometer march," Mengele replied.[61]

Apart from the fact that those young people had just completed a five-day trip in crowded freight cars with little food, water, or sleep, many of them chose to ride because they did not want to be separated from their families. Mengele's policies obviously had nothing to do with obtaining good workers for Germany. Workers were expendable; they could always be replaced. The same Nazis who were spending time and money in all the occupied nations to obtain non-Jewish laborers for work in Germany, and who were, in the process, driving young men into the Resistance, were murdering strong Jewish workers in the death camps. The Holocaust was a process beyond control: it was even against Germany's immediate material interests.

The 196 men and women who remained alive that Sabbath evening now addressed themselves to the problem of survival. They had been deliberately stripped of every personal possession—clothing, photographs, letters, books, mementos—that might tie them to their pasts. They had no families and no nationality; no past and no future. They had no identity but the numbers burned into their arms.

One man died almost immediately. Of the 148 remaining men, about half went to work at the coal mines of Jawiszowice, where the average life span for slave laborers was three months; 11 survived. Forty-two went to recover bricks from the rubble of the Warsaw ghetto; 3 survived. The rest stayed to work at Auschwitz. Of these, none seems to have survived.[62]

Even less is known of the women, for only 1 of the 47 who entered the labor camp survived. Settimia Spizzichino, age twenty-two, was separated from the other women and sent to Dr. Mengele's laboratories. She was subjected to so-called medical experiments until the end of the war. The Allies liberating Bergen Belsen found her still alive among a pile of corpses. Years later she told Robert Katz, "I felt more comfortable with the dead than with the living."[63]

In his excellent book about the October roundup published in 1969, Katz listed fifteen survivors with their professions and cities of residence.[64] One had since died and one had emigrated to Montreal. The remaining thirteen lived in Italy; all but one of these (Arminio Wachsberger, a chemical executive in Milan) still lived in Rome. The youngest boy to return was fifteen in 1943; three others were sixteen and three were seventeen. The oldest survivor was forty-four at the time of his arrest. He defied all odds, for men over forty rarely survived the first selection. A French Jewish inmate on the railroad platform at

The Italians and The Holocaust

Auschwitz whispered a warning to Wachsberger. "Tell the Nazis you are under thirty." [65]

News of the October 16 roundup spread through Rome quickly, even before the prisoners departed for Auschwitz. On Sunday, October 17, the day after the arrests, the Italian Resistance newspaper *L'Italia libera* informed Romans with remarkable prescience that "the Germans during the night and all day long went around Rome seizing Italians for their furnaces." [66] Nevertheless, not a single regular newspaper carried the story. Not a single Italian government official seems to have publicly protested the German action against Italian citizens. Worst of all, not a single word of public protest issued from the Vatican. Like other Italians, priests, monks, and nuns throughout Rome, and indeed, throughout the country, were hiding Jews at great personal risk to themselves. But from the Pope himself, there was only silence.

In fact, the Pope seems to have learned about the pending roundup by at least October 9, one week before it actually occurred. Eitel Friedrich Möllhausen, acting German ambassador to Rome during the temporary incapacity of Ambassador Rudolf Rahn, learned in September that Kappler had been ordered to arrest and deport the Roman Jews. He also knew that Kappler's orders said that the Jews were to be "liquidated." Möllhausen was horrified, both because he abhorred mass murder and because he believed that the action would provoke a public papal condemnation, with adverse consequences for the German war effort.

Among other steps, Möllhausen on October 6 informed Foreign Minister Joachim von Ribbentrop of the pending action and actually used the word "liquidated." He suggested that the Jews instead be kept in Rome and be used to build fortifications. [67] On October 9, Möllhausen received the answer he should have expected. He was told, in no uncertain terms, to mind his own business. [68] At that point, if not before, Möllhausen informed the German ambassador to the Holy See, Baron Ernst von Weizsäcker, who in turn told officials at the Vatican about Kappler's orders. [69] Those officials surely notified the Pope.

Apparently both Möllhausen and Weizsäcker believed that Vatican pressure behind the scenes could forestall the SS roundup. They were soon enlightened and disappointed. There is no evidence that Pope Pius XII ever acted on his knowledge. Before the roundup, he never threatened, suggested, or even hinted that he would publicly condemn any SS action to deport the Jews of his own city.

According to Möllhausen, Vatican officials learned of the pending roundup from Weizsäcker. Even if this account were untrue, however, it is unlikely that the Pope did not learn of the Nazi plan from other sources. Too many people knew. German diplomats attached to the embassy and to the Holy See, many of whom were Catholics and acquainted with German priests in Rome, knew. Some Italian police knew. Many Italian bureaucrats responsible for census data and ordered to provide the names and addresses of Roman Jews during the week before October 16 knew. It is inconceivable that the Pope himself, with his vast information network of priests and active Catholic laymen throughout Rome, did not know.

Furthermore, the Pope had been informed of the specific fate awaiting all deported Jews long before October 1943. Diplomatic representatives to the Holy See from several Allied nations and leaders of international Jewish organizations sent him reports of the Holocaust as early as September 1942. Like everyone else, he at first regarded the reports as wildly exaggerated Allied propaganda, and he was unwilling to become an Allied tool. But the reports kept coming in from different sources, and each new one confirmed the others. The truth was inescapable. [70]

The Italians and The Holocaust

By the end of 1942, the Pope had almost certainly received the graphic and detailed report of SS Colonel Kurt Gerstein, a disinfection officer who personally witnessed a mass gassing at Belzek in August. Gerstein had first attempted to contact Monsignor Cesare Orsenigo, the papal nuncio in Berlin, but he was turned away. He then delivered his report to a Dr. Winter, the coadjutor of Cardinal Count Preysing, archbishop of Berlin, with the request that it be forwarded to the Vatican.[71] Vatican spokesmen never denied receiving it.

Gerstein, a religious Protestant who joined the SS in the late 1930s solely to investigate rumors of the gassing of German mental patients, was a strange and enigmatic figure. His report, if unconfirmed by other sources, might have sounded like the ravings of a madman. But his report was not unconfirmed. It simply repeated, with more terrible precision, the information already given the Pope by diplomats and Jewish leaders.[72]

Eventually, churchmen from all of Europe also confirmed the reports. There were, after all, millions of German Catholics, many of whom served in the army and were aware of the massacres of Jews in the East. Thousands of Catholic priests also served in the army. What the priests did not learn for themselves, Catholic soldiers told them. Thousands of other Catholic priests lived and worked throughout Europe, in close contact with the people. They too learned part of the truth, both from their own experience and from at least some conscience-stricken parishioners. They passed information along to their superiors, and ultimately it reached the Vatican. New reports reaffirmed those already received.[73]

What might the Pope have done before October 16? A private threat to condemn publicly any SS action against Roman Jews probably would not have forestalled the roundup, but it would certainly have placed the Pope on sounder moral ground. In addition, the Pope might have made use of his knowledge by warning unsuspecting Jews who felt secure in part because of his very proximity. Either publicly or privately through the good will of thousands of priests, he might have sounded an alarm and saved thousands of lives. He, of all people, would have been believed.

Pope Pius XII, however, did not just fail to speak out or exert private pressure before October 16. He also failed to issue a public protest after the roundup had actually occurred. When the news of the raid reached him, he limited himself to permitting Bishop Alois Hudal, rector of the German Catholic Church in Rome, to write a mild letter to General Rainer Stahel, German army commander of occupied Rome. The letter, delivered in the early evening of October 16, said in part:

A high Vatican dignitary in the immediate circle of the Holy Father has just informed me that this morning a series of arrests of Jews of Italian nationality has been initiated. In the interests of the good relations which have existed until now between the Vatican and the German High Command . . . I earnestly request that you order the immediate suspension of these arrests both in Rome and its vicinity. Otherwise I fear that the Pope will take a public stand against this action which would undoubtedly be used by the anti-German propagandists as a weapon against us. [74]

Here at last was a private warning of the possible public condemnation that so many Germans dreaded. Weizsäcker believed the possibility to be very real, and in a message to the German Foreign Ministry in the earliest hours of October 17, he said so. He also declared, "People say that when similar incidents took place in French cities, the bishops there took a firm stand. The Pope, as supreme head of the Church and Bishop of Rome, cannot be more reticent than they." In the same message Weizsäcker suggested that the Pope's reaction to the arrests "could be dampened somewhat if the Jews were to be employed in labor service here in Italy." [75]

The Italians and The Holocaust

If the Pope ever had a chance to help Roman Jews, however, by October 16 it was too late. Bureaucracies react slowly. Eberhard von Thadden, a German Foreign Ministry official, sent a routine description of Hudal and Weizsäcker's communications to Adolf Eichmann, chief of the Gestapo section dealing with Jews, on October 23.[76] That day, over eight hundred Roman Jews were gassed and cremated at Auschwitz. Furthermore, the Pope never carried out his private threat. He never publicly condemned the deportation of the Jews who lived beneath his very windows.

Pope Pius XII's only public comment on the events of October 16 appeared in the Vatican newspaper *L'Osservatore Romano* on October 25–26, after most deportees were dead. The article said in part:

> As is well known, the August Pontiff, after having vainly tried to prevent the outbreak of the war . . . has not desisted for one moment from employing all the means in His power to alleviate the suffering which, whatever form it may take, is the consequence of this cruel conflagration. With the augmentation of so much evil, the universal and paternal charity of the Supreme Pontiff has become, it might be said, ever more active; it knows neither boundaries nor nationality, neither religion nor race.[77]

Ambassador Weizsäcker assessed the article in a message to the Foreign Ministry on October 28. Obviously relieved by the mildness of the Pope's comment, he wrote:

> Although under pressure from all sides, the Pope has not allowed himself to be drawn into any demonstrative censure of the deportation of the Jews of Rome. Although he must expect that such an attitude will be resented by our enemies and exploited by the Protestant circles in the Anglo-Saxon countries for the purpose of propaganda against Catholicism, he has done all he could in this delicate matter not to strain relations with the German Government and German circles in Rome.[78]

130

Rome, 1943: The October Roundup

After a brief analysis of the *L'Osservatore Romano* article, Weizsäcker concluded, "There is no reason whatever to object to the terms of this message . . . as only a very few people will recognize in it a special allusion to the Jewish question." Weizsäcker was wrong in that last conclusion, for many people undoubtedly understood the reference to "paternal charity" regardless of "religion or race." But he was right in feeling relieved. Pope Pius XII had hardly condemned a specific German action or warned others of pending danger.

Even a strong and immediate papal condemnation of the October arrests would have been too late for the 1,007 prisoners awaiting deportation and death. The Pope could not have saved them. For most Roman Jews still free after October 16, a papal warning to hide was no longer necessary. They now understood that they could be arrested at any time. Nor did hundreds of priests, monks, nuns, and Catholic laymen need the Pope to tell them to take in the Jews, because they were already acting. For most Romans, then, a papal condemnation after the event would have made little difference.

Outside Rome, however, the situation was different. Surprisingly enough, many Jews did not immediately learn about the October 16 roundup, or about raids in Milan, Turin, and Trieste during the same month. As will be seen, organized arrests of Jews in Florence, Genoa, Venice, and other cities with small Jewish populations did not begin until November or December. Many Jews continued to live at home or, at the very least, frequent Jewish institutions until that time. If the Pope had publicly said what he knew—if he had declared, clearly and unequivocally, that the Nazis were systematically deporting all Jews, without exception, in every country they occupied, and that once they had begun in any individual country, there was no reason to believe that they would limit their raids to just a few cities—many more people would have abandoned their homes and hidden. If he had added what he also knew—that the deportation trains were carrying Jews not to labor camps, as was the case with other Italians, but to certain death—people might have taken even greater precautions, and abandoned their jobs, their synagogues, and, if possible, even the cities where they could be recognized. After all, strong and healthy parents are much more likely to subject fragile grandparents and small children to the rigors of hiding if the alternative is annihilation rather than "resettlement."

Furthermore, while many courageous Italian Catholics sheltered Jews with no word of guidance from the Pope, still more might have done so if the head of the Church had clearly led the way, or if they had understood the full significance of the Holocaust.[79] In recognition of that fact, many Italian priests told parishioners, falsely, that the Pope had asked them to protect Jews. Also, a papal threat of interdict or excommunication might have led a few Italian Catholic policemen, militiamen, and bureaucrats serving Mussolini's Republic of Salò to think twice before arresting Jews. Even a few German Catholics might have hesitated. If only a few hundred lives had been saved, the effort would have been worthwhile.

Outside Italy, a strong papal condemnation of the Holocaust could have had an even greater impact. The Jews of Hungary, for example, were still free at the end of 1943. During the spring and summer of 1944, hundreds of thousands were arrested and deported by Hungarian officials who might have been influenced by the Pope. Even if he were not heeded, however, Pope Pius XII would, again, have been believed. His statement would not have been dismissed as enemy propaganda. Why did he not make the statement?

Several explanations of the Pope's behavior may be dismissed as unworthy and without foundation. Suggestions that he was in some way anti-Jewish and therefore insensitive to Jewish suffering are reprehensible. The Pope may have shared the prejudices of many Christians against Judaism as a religion, but there is no evidence that he did not grieve at the violence and horror of the Holocaust. Charges that he acquiesced out of personal fear are equally unworthy and lacking in evidence. A third explanation, that the Pope so feared bolshevism that he refused to condemn nazism, comes closer to the truth. Pope Pius XII was almost pathologically afraid of bolshevism. He loudly condemned Russian aggression in Finland, while ignoring German aggression in Catholic Poland. In Rome itself, he so feared a Communist takeover that on October 19, three days after the roundup, he actually requested the Germans to put more police on the streets. German police, who would also arrest Jews and, for that matter, anti-Fascist Christians, were the last thing the Romans wanted or needed.

But the Pope's anti-bolshevism does not adequately explain his reaction to the Holocaust. In fact, as he decided what to do that terrible October, Pope Pius XII faced several overwhelming problems. He knew that a strong public definition and condemnation of the Holocaust—the only reaction that might save lives—might cause the Germans to occupy the Vatican and invade churches and monasteries throughout Italy. In Rome alone, more than 450 Jews eventually hid in the enclaves of the Vatican, while more than 4,000 others found shelter in churches, monasteries, and convents. [80] Many thousands more hid in religious institutions throughout the country. Serious disintegration of German-Vatican relations could place these lives in jeopardy, without necessarily, in the Pope's view, saving others.

Second, the Pope feared that a condemnation of the Holocaust might provoke Nazi reprisals against Catholics in German-occupied countries, as well as even more terrifying persecution of the Jews. While it is difficult to imagine any more ferocious persecution than that already existing, it must be remembered that Catholic churchmen in several countries had been able to secure temporary exemptions from deportation for converted Jews and the children and Jewish spouses of mixed marriages. The Nazis sometimes granted these exemptions in order to buy silence from leaders of the Church, only to rescind them when all other available Jews had been deported. The Pope, however, did not want to jeopardize these private arrangements, especially when it remained unclear how many lives his condemnation of the Holocaust might save.

Third, Pope Pius XII was as concerned about his responsibility to preserve and protect an institution as he was about his moral leadership. He was well aware that Hitler toyed with the idea of establishing a rival papacy in Germany. He knew that the Vatican was completely at the mercy of the German troops occupying Rome. Above all, he had reason to believe that a large majority of German Catholics would reject any papal denunciation of the Holocaust. He feared that a threat to excommunicate Catholics who murdered Jews or to place Nazi Germany under interdict would result in a large-scale defection of German Catholics from the Church. Such a reaction certainly does not speak well of German Catholics, and perhaps it would not have occurred. The point here is that the Pope apparently believed it, and his belief influenced his policy. [81]

The fact that Pope Pius XII did not publicly condemn the Holocaust does not mean that he did nothing to help the Jews. The thousands of Jews hidden in religious institutions throughout Italy were there with his knowledge and consent, if not at his instigation. The hundreds of priests and even bishops in Italy who risked their lives to feed and shelter Jews were not discouraged by the head of their Church. But neither, apparently, were they particularly encouraged. The Pope seems to have chosen not to be involved even with priests inside the Vatican who were helping and supplying the persecuted. The best that can be said of him is that he allowed others to take great risks and that he fulfilled his institutional mandate at the expense of moral leadership.

And what of the Pope's most immediate flock—the Catholic population of Rome? What did they do after October 16? It is a twisted legacy. Hundreds of testimonies exist describing the revulsion and horror that ordinary Romans felt at the spectacle of the roundup. Most of these testimonies were written later, however, when the war was over and the truth of the Holocaust was known to everyone. They may be self-serving. Most people wanted to remember that they cared. It is difficult to know how many did.

Gestapo chief Kappler had no reason to distort the reaction of the Roman people when he composed his report of the roundup on October 17. He wrote:

> The behaviour of the Italian people was clear passive resistance which in some individual cases amounted to active assistance. In one case, for example, the police came upon the home of a Fascist in a black shirt and with identity papers which without doubt had already been used one hour earlier in a Jewish home by someone claiming them as his own. As the German police were breaking into some homes, attempts to hide Jews were observed, and it is believed that in many cases they were successful. The anti-Semitic section of the population was nowhere to be seen during the action, only a great mass of people who in some individual cases even tried to cut off the police from the Jews. In no case was there any need to use fire-arms. [82]

Kappler's report accords with the testimony of many Jewish survivors who remember the non-Jews who helped them. Several families received phone calls from non-Jewish friends on October 16, warning them of the danger that had not yet reached their buildings. [83] Others hid in non-Jewish homes and passed from home to home for the duration of the war. Non-Jews provided food, money, and false documents. [84] Luciano

The Italians and The Holocaust

Morpurgo remembers how his Catholic neighbor even fabricated false bills of sale to prove that Morpurgo's valuable furniture belonged instead to him, saving it from confiscation and returning it after the war. [85]

And yet, as always and everywhere, there was another side. Official newspapers not only failed to report the roundup, but avoided all mention of the sealed train winding its way north to the Brenner Pass, filled with Italian citizens. Fascist Italian diplomatic personnel, before the German invasion of their country, had tried to protect Jews throughout occupied Europe, but now bureaucrats at home seem to have done little for Jews on native soil. During the forty-eight hours that the prisoners were in the Military College, no one tried to free them. No one attempted to stop the deportation train as it crept slowly north toward the Brenner Pass. Perhaps if someone credible like the Pope had declared that for Jews deportation meant the gas chambers and crematoria, the public reaction would have been different. But perhaps it would not.

The lack of overt resistance was a measure of the Nazi terror, the disintegration of Italian authority, the difficulty of daily life for everyone in occupied Italy, and public ignorance about the Holocaust. Large-scale resistance to the deportations may have been too much to expect, and certainly the Italian record of passive resistance and spontaneous informal assistance to Jews is impressive. But here again, there was another side. Italian police did not participate in the October 16 roundup, in part because the Germans did not trust them and in part because of the still uncertain position of the new Italian national government at Salò. But as will be seen, at least 835 more Roman Jews were arrested before Rome was liberated in June 1944, and most of these were caught by Italian police. [86] Many were betrayed by Italian informers—individual citizens motivated by general anti-Semitism and pro-nazism, private quarrels and vendettas, their own personal involvement in illegal activities, or just plain greed. The Nazis offered rewards for information leading to the arrests of Jews, and several Italians collected. More often, the Germans received anonymous letters, such as the following:

> The Jew Benedetto Veneziano . . . a very rich textile merchant and real estate owner, is the owner of the following [three] automobiles [then listed with license plate and engine numbers].
>
> These cars have not been turned in at the proper collection center; on the contrary, with the tricks and corruption which only Jews know about, the owner has succeeded in obtaining permission to drive from the German command. . . .
>
> For more than a month the above-mentioned Jew has traveled the length and width of Italy to escape capture, using up gasoline and weaving intrigues. [87]

After providing more details, the informer signed his letter "A friend of Germany."

When the Germans finally retreated from Rome after nine months of occupation, at least 1,700 Jews arrested in Rome had been deported. [88] Over 10,000 had survived. Every survivor owed his life to one, and usually to several, heroic non-Jewish supporters. But except for those caught in that first, unexpected roundup in October, most deportees could also trace their tragedy to non-Jews who had, in the last analysis, failed to provide support.

The old buildings and narrow streets of the former ghetto still simmer beneath the hot sun, in the shadow of classical Roman ruins. Tiny shops still bear the same family names: Di Porto, Di Veroli, Spizzichino, Piperno, Limentani. The names evoke painful memories. Fifty-three men, women, and children named Di Porto, including three babies of six and seven months and fourteen other children ten and under, were deported to Auschwitz after the October 16 roundup. They were joined by forty-five Di Verolis, thirty-three Spizzichinos, thirty-one Pipernos, and sixteen Limentanis. None returned.[89]

The main synagogue in Rome still sits beside the Tiber adjacent to the ghetto, as it did when Foà's offices were there, and when Nazis seized its gold, archives, and library.[90] A plaque outside the synagogue and a room of prayer inside commemorate the Holocaust. After October 1982, a commemorative wreath marked another spot by the fence outside. Arab terrorists had launched an attack there, killing a two-year-old boy and wounding at least thirty-four others. Nazis had marched on that spot, and their Jewish victims had waited nearby for the trucks that would carry them on the first leg of their final journey. Forty years had passed, but hatred and fear had not entirely ceased.

7

Autumn 1943:
The Nightmare Begins

Dr. GIUSEPPE JONA, president of the Jewish Community of Venice since 1940, had been a well-known doctor, director of hospitals in Venice, and professor at the University of Padua before the racial laws. Denied the right to teach or hold a public position after 1938, he helped found a secondary school for Jewish students barred from government schools. He also worked with the thousands of refugees passing through Venice.

On Friday, September 17, only nine days after the unilateral Italian armistice with the Allies and the beginning of the German occupation, an unknown agent called upon the seventy-three-year-old Dr. Jona. The visitor demanded the lists of Community members. Dr. Jona, evidently well informed about the Holocaust in other countries, stalled for time. Perhaps he had learned the truth from the many refugees he knew, for little enough had yet occurred in Italy. The massacres of Jews around Lago Maggiore were underway, but he could hardly have known about them. German SS in Borgo San Dalmazzo had not yet demanded that all refugees from France surrender themselves on pain of death—they would do so the following day. Perhaps Dr. Jona had heard that the SS in Merano, a resort town near the Brenner Pass, had arrested twenty-five Jews, including a child of six, on September 15, but he could not have known that they would all be deported. Yet somehow Dr. Jona understood what lay ahead.

Calmly, Dr. Jona explained to his visitor that he needed time to collect the lists. Could he please return tomorrow? The man agreed. During the night, Giuseppe Jona collected and burned all documents bearing Jewish names and addresses. He never sought Italian police assistance. Instead, he injected himself with a lethal dose of morphine. Italy lost a distinguished public servant. She would lose more, many more. [1]

For most Italian Jews, September was a month of deadly quiet. As the German occupation forces solidified control and Mussolini's new Republican government (the king and Badoglio having become the traitors who signed the armistice) struggled to define its authority, hundreds of Jews silently abandoned their homes. Those with something special to hide usually went first. The Jewish American art critic Bernard Berenson left "I Tatti," his beautiful villa near Florence, a few days after the armistice. He found refuge with friends nearby. He somehow hid most of his vast art collection, along with about twenty thousand of his most valuable books. Another twenty thousand volumes remained behind. [2]

Letizia Morpurgo in Fano, with her husband and young children, left home in Trieste on September 10. Letizia's husband Giuseppe Fano had been director of Delasem in Trieste, and they believed that his position would make him a leading target for arrest. The Fano family fled to Venice, where they stayed for a time in hotels. They were not yet aware of the threat to all Jews, regardless of wealth or position, but they understood their own danger. That early knowledge, combined later with incredible good luck and heroic assistance from several sympathetic Italians, saved their lives. [3]

Like the Fano family, Pino Levi Cavaglione also left home in September because he feared he was a special target. Levi Cavaglione believed he was endangered as a Communist, rather than as a Jew. He had spent six years in prison and confinement during the Fascist regime. Released by the Badoglio government at the end of July 1943, he had returned to live with his parents in Genoa. The announcement of the armistice on September 8 was a cause for rejoicing, but the following day, German troops began disarming Italian soldiers.

On the evening of September 15, the chief of the political bureau of the Genoa police department came to call on the Levi Cavaglione family. He was, Pino recalls, the same agent who had arrested him six years before. This time his purpose was quite different. He warned Pino's father that the Germans intended to arrest the son the next morning.

Pino Levi Cavaglione promptly left home and found temporary refuge in a monastery. The monks, he remembers, were fully aware of his politics. Several days later, he traveled to Rome and joined a team of partisans in the Castelli Romani. He was still unaware of his vulnerability as a Jew. His parents remained at home for at least another month. By October 27, however, they too had changed names and moved to another house. They may have learned of the October 16 roundup in Rome from their partisan son or from their other son who was hiding with his family in a Roman convent. But despite their precautions, they did not survive. They were arrested on November 11, at the height of the Nazi manhunts in Genoa, and they disappeared in the vast inferno to the north. [4]

Another who went immediately into hiding in September

1943, for private reasons, was Ettore Ovazza, a fervent patriot, veteran of World War I, *squadrista*, participant in the march on Rome, and wealthy Turinese banker. During the late 1930s, Ovazza made a name for himself as a Jewish Fascist and anti-Zionist. In his newspaper *La nostra bandiera*, he constantly echoed the government's position that Zionists were disloyal and called upon all Italian Jews to condemn them. The official government favor he thus acquired enabled him and his followers to obtain leadership roles in the Jewish Community organizations, at the expense of Jews who were reluctant to disassociate themselves from Zionism. [5]

Unlike most others who fled early, Ovazza's move was not enough to save him, his wife, his twenty-year-old son, and his fifteen-year-old daughter. The family took refuge in the Valle d'Aosta, northwest of Turin and within view of the Swiss border. Early in October 1943, the German SS caught the son as he attempted to flee to Switzerland, and somehow discovered the family's hiding place. The SS murdered the boy and arrested his parents and sister. On the morning of October 11, in the cellar of an elementary school in Intra, north of Stresa, Ettore Ovazza, his wife, and daughter were shot. Their bodies were chopped into pieces and burned in the school furnace. The odor of burning flesh filled the air for days. Much later, a child playing near the furnace found a single human tooth. [6]

All who write of Ovazza agree that he was an honest man who acted in good faith. He understood what was happening in Germany in the 1930s. He sincerely believed that Italian Jews could prevent a similar fate only by demonstrating total devotion to fascism. It is true that, in the end, he died as a Jew under German, not Italian, domination. But the Duce he so loyally supported had abandoned him and his people several years before. Mussolini had used the Jewish question as a diplomatic tool. He had issued the racial laws, formed the alliance

Nazi, Fascist, and anti-Semitic graffiti on the walls of the synagogue in Trieste in December 1938, shortly after the onset of the racial laws. *CDEC, Milan.*

... official certificate of exemption
... most provisions of the racial laws,
...rded to Giacomo Tedesco "of the
...ish race" on August 23, 1941.
...sons for the exemption, unstated
...the certificate, may have included
...ntary military service, decoration
...bravery, or wounds received in
...bat in Libya, World War I,
...me, Ethiopia, or the Spanish Civil
...r; enrollment in the Fascist Party
...ween 1919 and 1922 or during the
...nd half of 1924; or wounds
...eived while fighting for the Fascist
...se in Italy. *CDEC, Milan.*

A store in Trieste in 1942, covered with graffiti declaring it "Closed forever. Jewish shop." *CDEC, Milan.*

Jewish forced laborers in 1942 working along the banks of the Tiber River in Rome, in the shadow of the Castel Sant'Angelo. *Publifoto, Rome.*

Forced labor card issued to "the Jew" Ada Levi in Cividali, of Bologna. The recipient was fifty-one years old and the mother of two children, both of whom were still minors. *CDEC, Milan.*

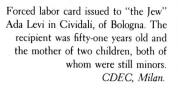

CONSIGLIO PROVINCIALE DELLE CORPORAZIONI
IN BOLOGNA

Cartolina-precetto N. 307

IL PREFETTO
Presidente del Consiglio Provinciale delle Corporazioni

Ai sensi delle disposizioni vigenti in materia di precettazione dei lavor... Per delega del Ministero delle Corporazioni;

PRECETTA

l'ebreo **Levi Ada in Cividali**

In attesa dell'avviamento al lavoro che sarà successivamente comunica... il suddetto ebreo deve tenersi a disposizione del C. P. C.

Ogni cambiamento di domicilio dovrà essere tempestivamente notifica... al suddetto Consiglio Provinciale delle Corporazioni.

Bologna, 14/9/42 XX°.

p. IL PREFETTO
Presidente del Consiglio Provinciale delle Corporazi...

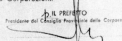

German SS announcement posted on September 18, 1943, in Italian villages near the mountain passes which led into southern France. The poster demands that all "foreigners" in the area around Borgo San Dalmazzo turn themselves in by 6 P.M., on pain of immediate death to themselves and all who might help them. About 349 Jewish refugees from France surrendered and, of these, 330 were deported to Auschwitz. *CDEC, Milan.*

MANDO GERMANICO
DI BORGO S. DALMAZZO

Entro le ore 18 di oggi tutti gli stranieri si trovano nel territorio di Borgo S. Dalmazzo e dei comuni vicini devono presentarsi Comando Germanico in Borgo S. Dalmazzo, SERMA DEGLI ALPINI.

Trascorso tale termine tutti gli stranieri non si saranno presentati verranno immediatamente fucilati.

La stessa pena toccherà a coloro nella abitazione detti stranieri verranno trovati.

Borgo S. Dalmazzo, 18 settembre 1943.

IL COMANDANTE GERMANICO DELLE S. S.
Capitano Müller

Barbed wire and guard tower at Fossoli, the main internment camp in Italy for Jews awaiting deportation to Auschwitz. *CDEC, Milan.*

Site of the crematorium in the prison of La Risiera di San Sabba, in Trieste. German soldiers trying to destroy evidence blew up the structure before abandoning the prison. *Italian postcard.*

Death cells in the internment camp at Gries, near Bolzano. Jews were held at Gries after the Nazis abandoned Fossoli in late July 1944. *CDEC, Milan.*

An anonymous informer's letter to Nazi or Fascist police. The text, full of errors, reads, "The Jew Joshua [Giosuè] who was at the Monti's house can be found hidden at Dottoressa Gentile's house in via Doria 9 [the Jew Joshua] has a wholesale shoe business in Milan." This letter led to the arrests of Augusta Menasse Voghera and her mother Giulia Voghera Leoni. Both were murdered at Gries in March 1945. *CDEC, Milan.*

Virginia and Leone Bondì with the three youngest of their six children. The entire family was caught in the Rome roundup on October 16, 1943, and gassed at Auschwitz a week later. *CDEC, Milan.*